Boyd Coddington's
How To Build
HOT ROD CHASSIS

D0556118

Timothy Remus

MBI Publishing Company

First published in 1992 by MBI Publishing Company,
PO Box 1, 729 Prospect Avenue, Osceola, WI
54020-0001 USA

© Timothy Remus, 1992

All rights reserved. With the exception of quoting brief
passages for the purposes of review no part of this
publication may be reproduced without prior written
permission from the Publisher.

The information in this book is true and complete to the
best of our knowledge. All recommendations are made
without any guarantee on the part of the author or
Publisher, who also disclaim any liability incurred in
connection with the use of this data or specific details.

We recognize that some words, model names and
designations, for example, mentioned herein are the
property of the trademark holder. We use them for
identification purposes only. This is not an official
publication.

MBI Publishing Company books are also available at
discounts in bulk quantity for industrial or sales-
promotional use. For details write to Special Sales
Manager at Motorbooks International Wholesalers &
Distributors, 729 Prospect Avenue, PO Box 1,
Osceola, WI 54020-0001 USA.

Library of Congress Cataloging-in-Publication Data

Remus, Timothy.
    Boyd Coddington's how to build hot rod chassis /
Timothy Remus.
        p.   cm.
    Includes index.
    ISBN 0-87938-626-6
    1. Hot rods—Chassis—Design and construction. I.
Title.
TL236.6.R458   1992
629.24—dc20   92-28517

On the front cover: A Boyd-built chassis with fully
independent front suspension. While being worked on
and moved about at the shop, the chassis is held at a
fixed height by strut rods, which will be replaced by coil-
over shocks.

On the back cover: Boyd Coddington (right) discusses a
chassis design with chassis builder Larry Sergejeff in the
Hot Rods by Boyd shop; repeated measuring before
welding ensures proper placement of suspension
components.

Printed in the United States of America

Contents

Acknowledgments

Time for a few thank-yous. At the top of the list is Boyd Coddington. The idea to do this series of books came out of a lunchtime conversation that Boyd and I had while working on the **Hot Rods of Boyd Coddington** book. We discussed the lack of good technical information and how that void might be filled—a means of providing detailed technical guidance to men and women who want to build their own street rods. So with Boyd's blessing and the encouragement of Motorbooks, we decided to create a set of building manuals for street rodders.

Boyd must be thanked for his encouragement and also for making his shop and offices available to me. His chassis-building wizard, Larry Sergejeff, must be thanked too. Larry never got tired of having me look over his shoulder (at least he never said so) and he never seemed to get tired of my endless questions. I must also thank Dick Brogdon at the Hot Rod shop for help with photos and scheduling.

The other shop that provided major assistance is Metal Fab in my home city of Minneapolis, Minnesota. It would have been nearly impossible to shoot all the photos needed for a book like this in one shop—especially when that shop is two thousand miles away. Jim Petrykowski offered to help fill the gaps in the photo record by allowing me to shoot some chassis work in his shop. Jim's offer to help was like being thrown a large lifesaver while floundering in stormy seas.

There are a few more people who helped in various ways or this relatively large project would never have been completed. Jim Prokop, a talented street rodder, proofread the book and suggested some necessary changes. Ralph Lisena of Engineered Components helped enormously with the chapter on brakes and did it without any strings attached.

Other manufacturers helped as well. Jerry Slover sent suspension kits to install and also provided help over the phone. The list is nearly endless—Chassis Engineering, JFZ, Aldan, everyone was willing to share their information.

Steve Hendrickson, the well-known editor of *Rodders Digest* magazine, must be thanked too for help with illustrations and a few missing photos.

Finally, I have to thank my lovely and talented wife, Mary Lanz. Month after month she puts up with my strange hours and even stranger paychecks. I couldn't do a book like this without the help of Boyd and Larry and Jim, and I certainly couldn't do it without Mary.

Introduction

This is the first in a series of four Boyd Coddington how-to tech books. The idea is to provide street rodders with a series of good technical manuals that will guide them through the building of their street rods. Chassis building is the focus of this first book, and it will be followed by a book on engines and drivetrains. Books three and four will deal with bodywork and body design, and painting. Our goal is to provide accurate, timely information in a format that anyone can understand.

This book is organized according to various parts of the chassis. The first chapter covers planning (the most important part of any project), followed by frame building and suspension chapters. There are also chapters on brakes, shocks, wheels, and even engine installation.

I feel there are two basic kinds of technical information—the theory behind the component or part (how it works), and the hands-on information (how to install it). Each chapter starts off with a theory section that includes a short discussion of various designs and a look at the various products on the market. The hands-on section discusses the real-life problems encountered when installing suspension systems, shock absorbers, an engine and transmission, and so forth.

In writing the book I tried to strike a balance. The material ranges from basic systems to relatively high-tech setups. From straight axle designs that date back to the first hot rodders to the newest systems to come out of shops like Hot Rods by Boyd. In tone I tried for a middle ground too, with language and discussions that anyone with a little mechanical aptitude could understand—yet without talking down to any of my readers.

Each chapter includes a number of photos and some illustrations intended to clear up most of the confusion that goes along with any good technical discussion. If a picture is worth a thousand words, then a really good illustration (I don't know if mine are *that* good) should be worth about ten thousand words.

At the back of the book is a sources section that lists most of the manufacturers and shops mentioned in the text.

If there's a personal reason for writing this book, it's to help a few street rodders avoid some of the nasty mistakes that I made in my early attempts at building hot rods. I remember well working in Mom and Dad's small garage—the late nights, the grease-soaked cigarettes, and the warm beer. What I've been trying to forget is the sometimes awful work that I did.

So if I can help street rodders build better cars and do most of the work themselves, well then it's all worth it. As long as we keep using our heads and our hands to design and build better and better street rods, the sport/hobby and its enthusiasts will continue to grow and grow.

Chapter 1

Planning

Introduction

Before describing the planning and building of a chassis for your new street rod, we should perhaps back up a bit and define the word chassis. For our purposes, the word chassis will include the frame, the suspension (both front and rear), the steering linkage and column, the brakes, and finally, the wheels and tires. The engine and transmission mounts will also be considered part of the chassis.

Theory

Building a Foundation, Bolt by Bolt

The chassis for your new street rod is a major part of the car. Jim Petrykowski, owner of Metal Fab in Minneapolis called the chassis "The foundation of your car—it's like the foundation of your house, everything else depends on it."

Like the foundation of your house, the chassis for your street rod must be laid up piece by piece. Any mistakes made during the construction of the

Building a great street rod requires careful planning. Here is a drawing to scale of a street rod frame at Hot Rods by Boyd. Like a blueprint, this drawing has all the essential dimensions.

chassis will be magnified later when you try to finish the project. If the frame isn't straight and square, the body won't fit correctly and the car won't sit correctly. Sloppy chassis work will affect more than just the fit of the body, it can also affect the way the car handles, the alignment, and ultimately the safety of your new vehicle.

The success or failure of your new street rod depends on more than your ability as a mechanic or the depth of your wallet. It also depends on your ability to think. Because building the chassis for your new car looks so exciting, most people just jump in and "do it." Planning is kind of like reading the directions—something you do when all else fails. Yet, a few hours spent on planning—before going out to buy all the sexiest parts in the world—will do more than anything else to ensure that the car you build meets all your expectations.

The Importance of Your Plan

So take the time, before starting, to put together a good plan for the street rod building project.

A good plan will: help you get the car you want, one that doesn't need major modifications after it's built; help ensure the money you spend is spent wisely and not wasted on fads or inappropriate parts; and help you build a car where everything works together in both a mechanical and aesthetic sense.

It might be easier to just start ordering parts. The temptation exists to assume we know what we want, and we rush off to do it. Taking the time to work through a plan is a harder, though ultimately much wiser, path to follow.

Hands-On

The Diagram of Your Car

By the time you are ready to build a chassis, you already know whether the car will be a Deuce coupe or a '38 Chevy sedan. If you haven't already, you need to decide on a few of the finer points about the car. Things like how low it will sit, and whether it will be a pro-street car with monster tires in the rear. You need to know what the wheelbase will be, what type of suspension you will use at both ends, how far back the motor will sit, and where the firewall will be.

With these basic parameters in mind you can start on the diagram of your car. This sketch doesn't need to be fancy, just neat enough so you can read all the measurements.

If you are "rebuilding" a current car or transforming an old stocker into a modern street rod, then take a measuring tape to the car before pulling it all apart. Park it on a clean piece of level concrete and start measuring. By knowing where everything is beforehand, you will be better able to determine where you want things to end up.

The sketch of your new car should include the essential measurements. The tires you use will determine the spindle height. Everyone wants their car low, but how low can you really go? By sketching everything out you can better determine what a dropped front axle and Model A cross-member will mean to the actual height of the frame rails and the oil pan.

Figuring the width of your new rod means coordinating axle dimensions with wheel size and offset. It's easy to get confused when trying to juggle wheel width and offset, and match those dimensions correctly with a given axle dimension. You're not through until you've made sure the tires won't rub

You don't have to be a draftsman but neat sketches of your car and chassis will help to focus your ideas and keep you on track during the building process. A set of drawing tools like these will help with the sketch—and they're great when you have to make a template or pattern for any parts you're fabricating.

on the frame or the outer fender lip. Once again, the sketch will help clear up any confusion.

Figuring out the wheelbase might seem the simplest part of the project. Like a lot of things, it ain't as simple as it might seem—especially if your new car will be full fendered. In a nutshell, many cars

If you want it "in the weeds," then plan it that way. Build it low, don't build it and then drop it. Rodder's Digest

Name of Customer _____

Make of Car _____ Model _____ Year _____

Wheelbase Stock	=
Track Width Front	=
Track Width Rear	=
Axle Flange to Flange Front	=
Axle Flange to Flange Rear	=
Wheel Size Front	=
Wheel Size Rear	=
Tire Size Front	=
Tire Size Rear	=
Tire Ø Front	=
Tire Ø Rear	=
Tire Width Front	=
Tire Width Rear	=
O.D. Tire to O.D. Tire Front	=
O.D. Tire to O.D. Tire Rear	=
O.D. Fender to O.D. Fender Front	=
O.D. Fender to O.D. Fender Rear	=
Clearance Width inside Fender Front	=
Clearance Width inside Fender Rear	=
Ground to top of inside Fender Front	=
Ground to top of inside of Fender Rear	=

Center Front Axle	=
Center Rear Axle	=
Bumpers	=
Floorboard (Angle and Height	=
Firewall	=
Firewall to Radiator	=
Front Crossmember	=
Rear Crossmember	=
X - members	=
Brake Pedal assembly location	=
Gas Tank Location	=
Gas Tank Measure	=
Car has Independent or Solid Axle Front	=
Car has Independent or Solid Axle Rear	=
Sway Bar Front	=
Sway Bar size Front	=
Swaybar Rear	=
Swaybar size Rear	=

Tire to top of inside Fender Front	=
Tire to top of inside of Fender Rear	=
Ride Height Front Frame	=
Ride Height Rear Frame	=
Ride Height Body Front(	=
Ride Height Body Rear (	=
Ground to top of Fender Weld Front	=
Ground to top of Fender Weld Rear	=
Lowest part Fender to ground Front	=
Lowest part Fender to ground Rear	=
Frame Width over Axle Front	=
Frame Width over Axle Rear	=
Tire Clearance-track width to inside Fender Front	=
Tire Clearance-track width to inside Fender Rear	=
Fender Weld Lip width Front	=
Fender Weld Lip width Rear	=
Axle Clearance to Frame Front	=
Axle Clearance to Frame Rear	=

Wheelbase for best wheel fit	=
Front Axle Forward	=
Front Axle moved back	=
Rear Axle Forward	=
Rear Akle moved back	=
Car can be lowered over all	=
Front	=
Rear	=
Fire Wall to be cut back of not	=
Engine	=
Trans	=
Shifter	=
Wheel size Front	=
Wheel size Rear	=
Tire size Front	=
Tire size Rear	=
Brand Wheels	=
Brand Tires	=

Great hot rods don't just happen. They are the result of meticulous planning. Here's an example of some planning sheets used at Hot Rods by Boyd. For each project car the shop builds, a planning sheet of at least four pages of details is used, and many times there's much more information put down on paper before actual building starts.

Making the car sit just right isn't as easy as it might seem. It needs to be at the right height, usually lower in the front, and the wheels have to be centered in the fender open- *ings. It's a situation where everything clicks for the viewer and it doesn't happen unless you plan to make it happen (even then, it might not happen). Rodder's Digest*

came stock with the rear tires—and sometimes the fronts as well—pretty far forward in the wheelwell. As the car gets lower and the tires get bigger, the effect is magnified.

To make matters even more confusing, spring and suspension kits don't all use exactly the same wheelbase. Some kits "correct" a little to move the rear axle farther back in the wheelwell while others use strictly stock dimensions. There is no easy answer. You need to understand what you want, where you want the tire to be in the fender well, and how to achieve that tire position. If you are buying a four-bar kit or Mustang suspension, ask the manufacturer if the kit uses stock dimensions. More important, ask where the wheels will end up in the fender opening. If possible, tack weld in the suspension and then set the body and fenders on for a look-see.

A wealth of information on "what works" and what doesn't is available at any rod run. Take a minute to look over the cars that look like yours. If they're really low, note the components used to get them that low, how the components were mounted, and where that leaves critical elements like the oil pan. As one local builder said: "Look under some of

Let's see, a hot rod needs to be raked just right, it should be low, the rear tires should be big. Gee, everything's here—and it took a lot of work to make it that way. In particular, remember that big tires affect the gear ratio and the rear braking. If you build it level and drop the nose later, then the caster angle is way off. So plan it right the first time. Rodder's Digest

Another case where everything turned out extremely well. A little extra time spent at the beginning of the project will pay big dividends later when the car comes out looking right the first time. Rodder's Digest

those cars at the rod runs and see how many have the rear four-bar adjustments screwed out as far as they will go—because they're trying to move the tire farther back in the fender well."

The sketch of your car should show clearly:
● Spindle height front and rear (tire diameters/two)
● Wheelbase
● Height of the frame rails at the corners and their lowest point
● Height of the engine oil pan
● Side view of where the four bars or ladder bars or locating links locate on the frame rails
● Track width front and rear
● Clearance between tires and the frame or fenders
● Axle flange-to-flange distance front and rear
● Offset of the wheels
● Distance between top of axle(s) and the frame (and will you need to "C" the frame at the back?)
● Location of the firewall (will it be recessed?) and location of the engine in the frame

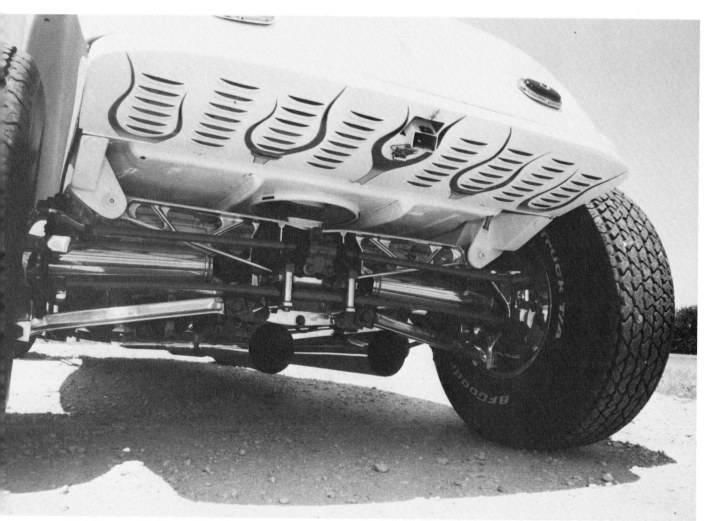

Certain cars call for certain solutions. Yes, the chrome-plated independent suspension is worth every nickel on this car. Rodder's Digest

For some cars, the type of rear suspension isn't nearly as important. Note the way the exhaust is routed to clear the triangulated four-bar suspension. Rodder's Digest

A timeless design; four-bars and tube axle are hard to beat, especially on an early car.

Some general, real-world, minimum distances might run as follows. Most of these are courtesy of Larry Sergejeff, chassis man at Hot Rods by Boyd in Stanton, California, for some seven years now.

Between the top of the rear axle and the frame, you need at least 3in before the axle hits the stop. If you want the car ultra-low, you will probably want to C the frame to provide enough clearance here. Between the frame and the ground you need at least 4in at the lowest point (usually along the frame behind the tire). That most vulnerable of compo- nents, the oil pan, should have at least 5in of clearance before it hits terra firma.

All these dimensions are taken at ride height. Ride height is the height of the car or components when it is fully finished, filled with gas and oil, and ready to run.

Once you have a good sketch of the car and the chassis with wheelbase, spindle heights, firewall location, and all the rest, you can progress to ordering parts and the actual construction.

Larry Sergejeff (left) and Boyd Coddington talk over plans for a new car whose chassis is on the table before them. Detailed planning is essential to successfully building a chassis. It's relatively easy to make changes while you're in the planning and measuring stage. The further along a project gets, the harder—and more expensive—it gets to make changes.

Boyd Coddington, whose cars have won great critical praise and numerous major awards, understands the vital need to thoroughly plan out a project before any metal is even measured or cut. Making changes on paper is easy; it gets harder to make changes once metal is cut and welded.

Chapter 2

Building the Frame

Theory

I'd Rather Do It Myself

This chapter is intended for the street rodder who wants to build a frame, starting with a bare set of frame rails. Some street rodders might wonder why a person should go to all this work when complete frames are already available. Each builder will have his or her own answer of course, but there are a number of advantages to constructing your own frame. First is cost. By purchasing a set of rails and fabricating your own cross-members (or even buying the cross-members too) there is usually a significant savings. Second, some professional builders start with rails so they don't have to worry that a complete frame—though it might have been perfectly straight and true when it left the factory—was "tweaked" slightly during shipping. Third, by building your own frame you can have whatever you want, be it pro-street or a longer wheelbase, or rails that are pinched slightly in front.

Frame Designs

They call the single leaf spring on the front and back of Henry Ford's early cars a "buggy" spring because it was borrowed directly from the horse-drawn buggy that preceded Henry's automobiles. Those horse-drawn buggies used a very simple frame made up of two wooden rails that ran the length of the buggy, with cross-members used to tie the two side rails together.

When Henry and others hung a motor on those first buggies, they kept the simple wooden frame. When the stress of high-speed driving proved too much for those early rails, they were simply swapped for steel, though the basic design remained. Today, some eighty years later, street rodders are still working with (usually) a simple ladder frame made of steel rails with steel cross-members.

Besides the inherent weakness of the wood, those early frames had another large drawback: their shape. A box or rectangle doesn't have much structural integrity. Henry was one of the first to realize that by placing a series of triangles—known today as an X-member—in the center of the frame.

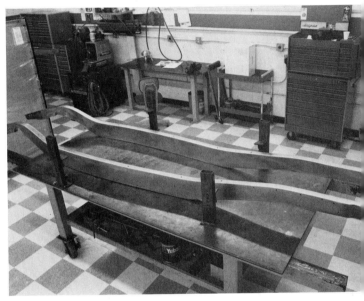

It all starts with a set of rails, a table and four sturdy stands. These rails are from SAC, the shop is Hot Rods by Boyd. The idea is to get the rails up on the stands at the approximate ride height.

He got about ten times the strength with only a little extra weight.

As time went on, more and more of the early automobiles got X-members in the center of their rectangular frames. This was done to help those cars deal with the additional weight and horsepower that came along with the other advancements of the automobile. The side rails became stronger too. As time went on the side rails became taller, going from the 3in or 4in tall rails of a Model A to the 5in or 6in tall rails of the '46 Ford. As the side rails became taller, they tended to be reinforced and partly "boxed" in order to add even more strength.

Today, a street rodder building a frame can follow the same evolutionary path used by early car builders and designers. As the weight and horsepower of your car increases, the frame may need to be reinforced, often by the same means used many years ago.

13

The next step is to bolt in the front and rear cross-members or spreader bars. Spreader bars purchased for the frame have the advantage of being the correct dimension.

More Planning

This chapter is designed to aid the individual building a frame from a set of rails. Whether those rails are Henry's own or a new pair from SAC or Just A Hobby, you still need to construct some kind of jig to hold everything in the correct positions so that cross-members can be fabricated and welded in. The sketch you did as part of the planning process will ensure that you understand what you want: how low, how long, and how fat you want your new car to be.

If you bought the rails from a street rod manufacturer be sure that their dimensions agree with the dimensions on your sketch. Most manufacturers of street rod chassis and chassis parts provide diagrams that show the location of body mounting holes, cross-members, suspension mounting points, and axle centerlines.

If the rails lying on the floor of your shop are from Henry Ford or perhaps Louis Chevrolet, then reference diagrams are available that show the

Larry Sergejeff has bolted in a temporary cross-member at the front of the frame and is double-checking the width. Never assume a component is the correct dimension, always check and double-check all dimensions. Remember that when you ass-u-me anything you run the risk of making an ass out of u and me.

A large carpenter's T-square is a handy tool for checking the height of the frame. It should also be used to ensure that the rails don't twist as the cross-members are bolted and welded in place.

location of axle centerlines and body mounting holes. If the body you plan to set on the frame is a fiberglass body, you might want to contact the body manufacturer. Some fiberglass bodies fit better than others and the manufacturer might have a tip or two that will make everything come together more easily down the road.

Frame Rails and Cross-Members—Component Selection

Most aftermarket rails are made from mild steel, flame-cut, and then welded together in a jig. The accuracy of these rails is dependent on the jigs and the skill of the men and women who do the cutting and welding. It pays to ask around to get some feel for the quality of the various offerings.

Cross-members are usually more than mere channel iron punched with a few holes. Many of the frames for later cars are designed to carry a hefty cross-member. The basic triangle is an extremely

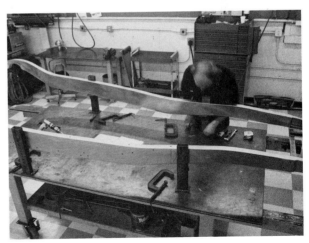

Sometimes the position of the stands must be adjusted before the rails are clamped in place. Be sure the stands don't end up getting in the way of welding and suspension mounting that will be done later.

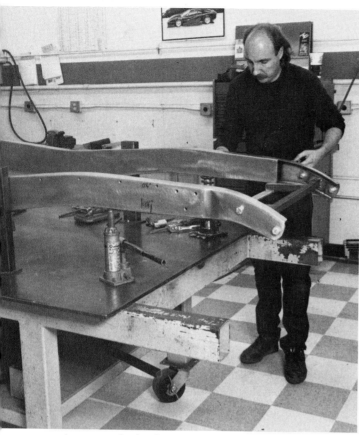

Larry uses hydraulic or screw jacks to do the final height adjustments of the frame rails. After the rails are exactly where he wants them, Larry puts shims between the rail and the stand and then clamps the frame rails in place.

Larry doesn't want these frame rails to move—not at all—so he uses serious C-clamps to hold everything in place. You can see the shim he placed between the stand and the rail.

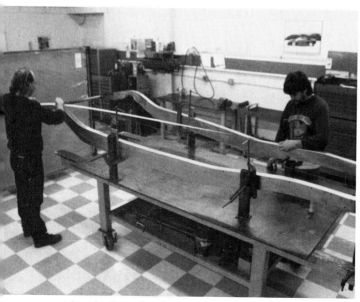

After the frame has been bolted in place, Larry checks the crisscross measurements to ensure that the frame is square. Use good reference points or create your own, based on the axle centerline and the distance from the frame centerline.

Larry likes to find and mark the axle centerlines early in the process. The centerlines are used as references for much of the construction and fabrication to follow. Next he will mark the location of the front cross-member.

Here, small plates are clamped to the bottom of the frame rails as an aid in mounting and welding in the front cross-member. The cross-member will sit on the small "shelf" created by the plate on either side of the frame rail.

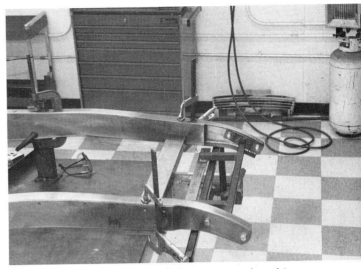

The front cross-member is made from rectangular tubing. Cross-members should be mild steel, at least 0.095in thick, although 0.120in is good if the load will be heavier.

strong shape, and an X member adds a great deal of strength for only a small penalty in weight. The strength and design of the cross-members will depend on the weight and the use you have planned for the car. A pro-street Deuce with a big-block Chevy will need more cross-member than a near-stock Deuce sedan equipped with a flathead.

If fabricating a complete X-member is beyond your level of skill, you can still build you own frame since complete cross-members are available. In addition to stocking standard cross-members, most frame rail manufacturers will do special orders. If you have special needs, such as a longer-than-stock wheelbase, most manufacturers are happy to comply. When you call and order the rails and other frame components, remember that the frame acts as the foundation for your car—buy the best quality you can find. The more uniform and accurate the rails and cross-members are, the easier it will be to construct a complete frame that is straight and square.

The cross-members themselves, whether home built or from the aftermarket, should be made from mild steel, at least 0.095in thick. As the car gets heavier and the loads increase, 0.120in mild steel is preferable with 0.120in chromoly used for the very toughest situations. Chromoly, that magical material we hear so much about, is indeed much tougher than mild steel. Larry Sergejeff, the chassis man at Hot Rods by Boyd, insists that all brackets and suspension mounting points be built from chromoly. Larry feels that "the chromoly is much more durable and the extra durability gives you some nice insurance when the frame is overloaded—like in an accident. The other thing that's good about chromoly is that a loose mounting bolt in a chromoly bracket won't 'eat' the bracket like it will if the bracket is built from mild steel."

The down side of chromoly, of course, is that it should be heli-arc welded for a clean and durable weld.

After the front cross-member is welded in place, it's time to check and adjust the width through the middle of the frame. These carpenter's clamps are a good way to pull the sides of the frame in slightly. Note that the centerline of the frame has been marked with a string that runs from the front cross-member to the rear cross-member.

After the cross-members are installed, Larry makes up an X-member from mild steel tubing 0.120in thick. The driveshaft is set in place to make sure there's enough clearance between the cross-members and the shaft.

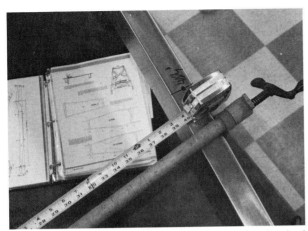

The width through the center of the frame can be checked against data supplied by the original manufacturer or the dimensions supplied by the manufacturer of the frame rails. Here the dimensions have been marked on the rails for easy checking.

Hands-On

The Actual Building—It All Starts with the Table

Constructing a quality frame that is straight and true requires a set of jigs, or more likely, a surface table. A surface table is just that, a table with a perfectly flat surface. Not to be confused with the floor of your garage, this table will allow you to set up two rails that are both at the same *exact* height. You won't have to wonder whether they are both at the same height because they were both measured from the table—the one that's flat and level.

Not everyone has a surface table and not every street rodder has enough garage space to build one that will just "sit around" after it's constructed. The answer is a table like the one at Metal Fab. Really just a framework of rectangular tubing with bolt-on legs, it serves the same purpose as a surface table, though the design allows you to disassemble the table and set it over against a wall when you're not using it. The important thing is to get the top surface as level as possible and make sure that each leg is equipped with a height adjustment so the whole table can be leveled out. This will provide you with a known reference point during the construction of your frame.

Next, you need four sturdy stands, one for each corner of the new frame. How elaborate these stands are depends on personal taste and skill. Some builders just tack weld the rails to the stands once everything is in position. The important consideration is that once the frame rail is bolted or tack welded to the stand, it doesn't move—not at all. The stands must be positioned so as not to interfere with the mounting of suspension components later.

Once you have the table and the stands, it's pretty much a matter of setting the two rails up on the stands and gradually working them up to the

A tubing bender is a handy tool here—making it possible to create bends of almost any radius. If you don't have one in your shop at home, you can probably get tubing bent at the local fabrication shop or even a muffler shop.

Each piece of the X-member is cut to fit and tack welded in place before the whole thing is final welded.

19

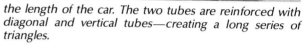

An inside look at Boyd's Aluma-Coupe designed by Larry Erickson. This is a good study in chassis design. The side "rails" are actually two long pieces of tubular steel that run the length of the car. The two tubes are reinforced with diagonal and vertical tubes—creating a long series of triangles.

right height. The right height here is "ride height." The distance from the bottom of the rails to the table should be the same as the height of the frame rails to the ground when the car is completely finished—gassed up and ready to roll. You are going to weld up the rails and cross-members, and install most of the suspension components (without the springs) as though the car were in fact, sitting on level ground.

The idea is to design and build the car at the ride height you want. You can't just lower the car after it's built or all your planning, not to mention suspension geometry, will go down the tubes. Your sketch and the information provided by the rail manufacturer is essential in setting up the frame rails, getting everything welded together, and attaching all the suspension components. The idea is to set the rails on the stands, bolt in cross-members or spreader bars, and then gradually work the two rails up to the perfect height.

Larry likes to use spreader bars designed for the car as he's sure these are the correct dimension. He also recommends buying rails with the full front horns, even if you intend to cut off the horns later. With the frame horns in place it's easy to bolt in a

At left
Another look at the Aluma-Coupe, this time from the back. Engine will be a four-cylinder turbo set just ahead of the rear axle. Once again there are a lot of triangles created with tubular steel.

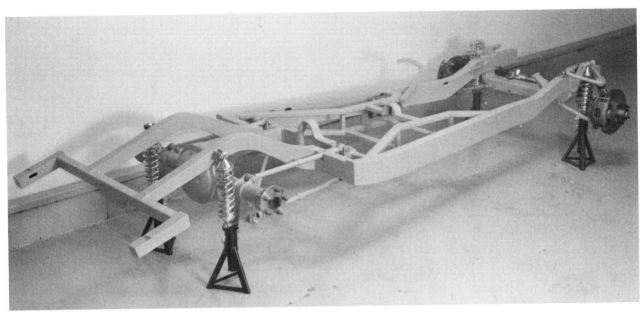

Complete frames are available from a number of manufacturers in a number of styles. This pro-street frame with independent front suspension is from Fat Man Fabrications.

spreader bar and get a quick start on the construction.

Getting Everything Perfect

With the rails at roughly the right height and with spreader bars clamped in at the front and rear of the frame, you should spend some time with a tape measure and a level (the new electronic ones work well here) making sure that everything is perfect. Be sure that the two corners at either end of the frame are at the same height, and that when the level is run across from one rail to the other it isn't "half a bubble off."

Making sure the frame is square will require a helper. Simply make sure that when you measure the frame from corner to corner, in crisscross fashion, the measurements are exactly the same. Use two different measuring points to double-check your measurements. If they come out exactly the same, then you know the frame is square.

Jim Petrykowski advises street rodders to use good, accurate measuring points when working on the frame: "A lot of builders use the body mounting holes, and that's not a good idea. On some cars those holes just aren't very accurate. I tell people not to worry about the body holes but rather to use reference holes in the frame—like the 'suspension bumper' holes in Ford frames located at the axle centerlines. These holes were used to hold the frames correctly as they moved down the line at the Ford plant.

"If builders are using holes in the top of the rail, (such as body mounting holes) at least be sure that all the holes are the same distance from the edge of the rail."

Photographed at Metal Fab in Minneapolis, this table is a good alternative to the massive surface tables used at Hot Rods by Boyd. The legs on this table bolt on, so the unit can be disassembled and stored out of the way. Note that each leg has an adjustment for height. The bracket on the end is a separate piece created to hold a particular style of frame.

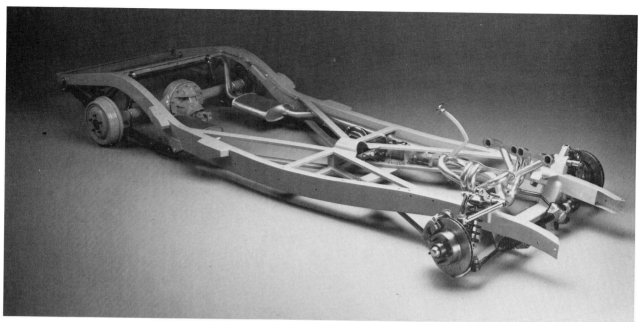

This 1935-40 Ford chassis is from Total Cost Involved (TCI) and carries its own independent front suspension utilizing tubular upper control arms and coil-over shocks. This chassis is available in four stages of completion (stage four is shown).

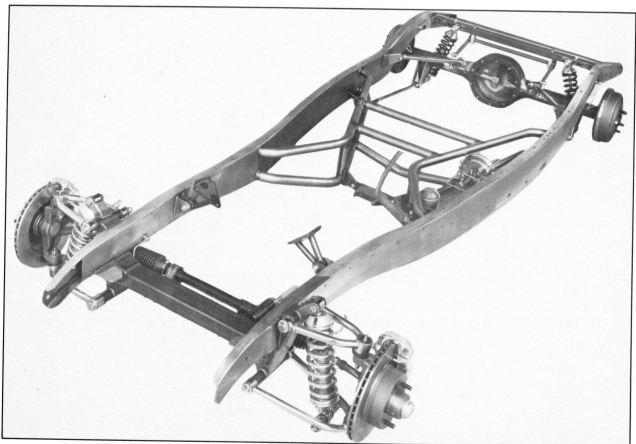

This 1933-34 Ford frame is from Heidt's and carries its own Superide independent front suspension with tubular A-frames, and a rear-steer rack and pinion. Disc brakes are standard, as is the tubular X-member to make it easier to route the exhaust.

If in doubt, you can make your own reference points, along the axle centerline at each corner. Just be sure each reference point is the same distance from the centerline of the frame.

Now you know that the frame is at ride height, that it is level from one side to the other, that it is set at the correct width at the front and back, and that it is square. If the rails you're using are originals, then you probably want to do some boxing. Larry Sergejeff recommends that early unboxed or partially boxed frames be boxed with material that is the same thickness as the frame itself, probably 0.120in plate. Frames need to be boxed in the center where the X-member mounts and all the way forward, past the point where the engine mounts attach to the frame. If the car is heavy or built for the fast lane with a big-block Chevy, then you probably want to box the entire length of the rails.

Like a lot of jobs, the job of building your frame relies mostly on careful setup and preparation for a good result. Once everything is set up correctly on the table, the rest of the cross-members can be welded or bolted into place. Original diagrams or the diagrams supplied by the rail manufacturer will be your guide to the exact placement of the cross-members. Be sure to watch for a twist in either of the rails as you weld in the cross-members. A T-square set on the table can be run along the rails occasionally to make sure they haven't started to twist.

Next, the side-to-side measurements through the center of the frame need to be checked against your diagram. The rails can be pushed out slightly with a porta-power unit or pulled in with a carpenter's clamp, and then the center cross-members can be welded in place (be sure the cross-members will clear the driveshaft).

Conclusion

After double-checking all your measurements and carefully welding everything in place, you've got a complete frame sitting on the table. Because the frame is sitting at ride height, you don't need to move a thing. The next step is much more exciting—actually mounting the suspension components.

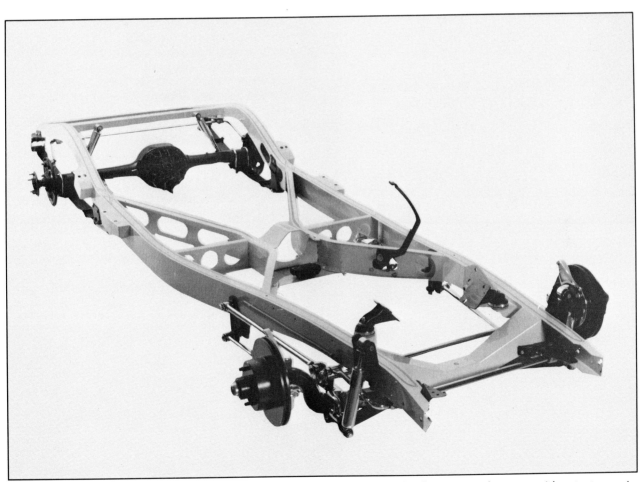

Another Ford chassis, this 1933-34 frame is from the Chassis Engineering crew. Though it is shown with a four-bar, the same chassis can be ordered with an independent suspension at the front. Note the way the front of the X-member has been opened up to provide extra transmission clearance. Chassis Engineering also has a new torsion bar independent suspension of their own design.

Chapter 3

Front Suspension and Steering

Introduction

This is the biggest chapter in the book, with a wealth of information. In organizing the book it seemed unnatural to separate front suspension from steering, since they are so intimately connected. Thus, the two subjects are presented together here, with the suspension section first followed by the steering section.

The hands-on part of this chapter follows the installation of three different styles of front suspension: A Boyd-built independent, a Mustang II kit, and a four-bar with a straight axle.

Theory—Front Suspension

How to Make an Intelligent Decision—The Criteria

The variety of suspension systems available for your street rod are almost endless. They range from

boring and stock to ultra-modern and sexy. Trying to make sense of it all and deciding which system is best for your car is no easy task. First we need some criteria by which to judge the various front suspension systems.

At the top of the list (at least at the top of mine) is money. You need to consider how much each system costs and exactly what you are getting for those hard-earned greenbacks.

Next is looks, sometimes called sex appeal. This subject is really more than just a matter of visual appeal. Some cars, early cars done in a traditional style for example, just don't look right with independent suspension. In reverse, a real high-tech Boyd-built car might not look good with a dropped straight axle. Considering looks means considering the style of the car you are building and then choosing a suspension system that fits both your wallet and your style.

How do you intend to use the car and how sophisticated are your tastes? How do you want it to handle? If your other two cars are Corvettes, and you want the new street rod to handle like a Corvette, then you'd better step up to full-tilt independent suspension.

Height. You need to consider height because as Larry Sergejeff is always saying, "You can only get a car with an independent front end to run so low, a car with a straight axle can run just a little lower."

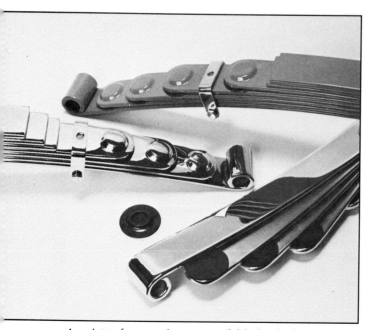

A variety of new springs are available for the front and rear of most popular street rods. These Super Slide springs with the moly-nylon pads are from Posies and come in various lengths and finishes, with or without reversed eyes. Posies

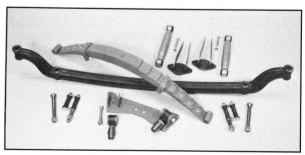

Posies manufactures this "In Da Dirt" kit in variations to fit 1935-40 and 1941-48 Fords. The kit includes the dropped front axle, Posies' Super Slide springs, shock kit, and wishbone split kit. Posies

Four-bar kits are available from a number of suppliers to fit a wide range of cars. These four-bars are from Pete and Jake's, designed for Model Ts. Tube or I-beam axles can be used, but you need to specify which axle you intend to use when ordering the kit. Pete and Jake's

Finally you need to consider the fit. Despite what some manufacturers might say, not every aftermarket suspension system will fit every street rod. In particular, only a few will fit correctly under the front fenders of early Ford and Chevy street rods.

Suspension Design—Which is Best

The first cars were little more than motorized buggies, and the earliest front suspension systems can be traced back to those covered wagons. In examining the pros and cons of various suspension designs, it might be best to start off with the simplest systems and then move on to the high-zoot, fully independent systems.

Straight axle, split wishbones: Henry had the old buggy in mind when he designed the early straight axle and wishbone. He designed a straight axle supported by a buggy spring and held in place by the "wishbone" that attaches to the axle at either end and then comes back to a common locating point, thus the name. The wishbone kept the axle from moving front to rear and also provided some lateral support.

The wishbone was a fine engineering concept, but left darned little room for Chevy V-8s with deep-sump oil pans. To provide a little more room under the engine some early hot rodder cut off the

wishbone at the common locating point and suddenly had two wishbones. With a little heat from the magic wrench, he (it's doubtful that it was a she at that early date) soon had each wishbone located to the frame rail instead of the common locating point.

He now had more room for engine swaps in that early hot rod, though he hadn't done much for the handling or geometry. When one wheel of a split system encounters a bump or driveway, it pivots on the long wishbone—experiencing a caster change as

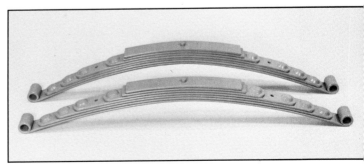

You can put it in the weeds with these front springs from Posies, designed for 1928-34 Fords. With less arch these springs help to get the car low without compromising the ride. Posies

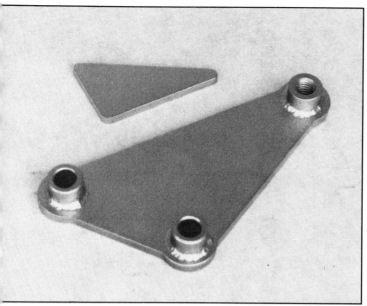

Vega steering gears are popular for street rodders who want cross-steer geometry without power steering. A mounting plate like this one from Pete and Jake's makes mounting the Vega gear to your frame much easier. Pete and Jake's

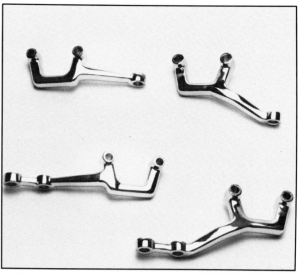

Different front axle configurations require different steering arms to clear tie rods and four-bars. These forged arms are from Chassis Engineering, designed to fit 1935-48 Fords with a dropped axle. When ordering parts you have to be sure to coordinate all the parts so they work together. Chassis Engineering

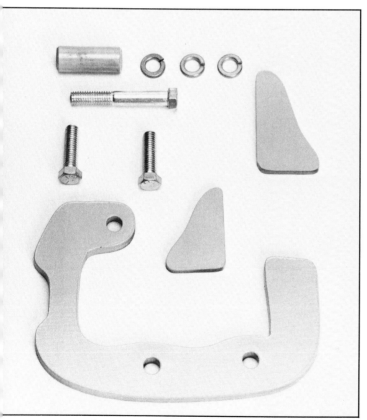

Another means of mounting a Vega gear to the frame rail is offered by this Chassis Engineering mounting plate. The plate is welded to the left frame rail and moves the gear closer to the rail than most other designs. Chassis Engineering

it does so—while the other wheel rides along without any change. What this does is place a twist on the axle. (This is why some people say a split wishbone suspension should only be used with an I-beam or forged axle and not with a tubular axle.) A better system would allow each wheel to move up or down without twisting the axle and without any caster change.

Straight axle, four-bar setup: Made famous by Pete and Jake's, the four-bar or four-link system uses two "links" on each side to hold the axle in place. When one wheel encounters a bump, it moves up, the bars act as a parallelogram-type linkage, and there is no caster change and no twist on the axle. The wheel does move back and forth slightly as it goes over a bump.

The four-link system has a number of advantages when compared to its evolutionary predecessor. Because each wheel operates somewhat more independently of the other, the ride is improved and a given bump has less tendency to upset the entire suspension. The other advantage is in the appearance of the four-bar system. A chrome-plated four-bar setup has a great deal more sex appeal than that funky old stuff of Henry's (disregard this comment if you're after the nostalgia look).

A four-bar can also be run with a coil-over at either end in place of the buggy spring. This is a system that is only now gaining in popularity, though it works quite well. The coil-overs help to further improve the ride of the old straight axle and also make it easy to adjust the height or change the spring rates. Most of these systems come out of shops like Boyd's and Metal Fab in Minneapolis.

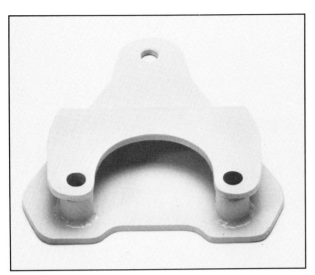

Traditionalists will appreciate this wishbone mounting kit. The kit allows you to mount an unsplit wishbone lower than stock—providing clearance for stick and Ford C-4 transmission installations. Chassis Engineering

More and more street rodders are putting sway bars on the front and rear of their cars—thus more and more manufacturers are offering sway bar kits. This front bar is from Chassis Engineering, designed to fit 1935-40 Fords. Chassis Engineering

When Henry started all this business, he relied on the wishbone to help locate the axle laterally. When the wishbones are split or replaced by four-links, the only thing locating that axle side to side is the buggy spring itself. That's why most manufacturers of these systems recommend the use of a panhard rod to locate the axle side to side.

Straight axle, parallel leaf springs: Some of Henry's competitors over on the other side of town had different ideas about springs and such. They used two long leaf springs to support and locate the straight axle. The major disadvantage here is sex appeal—the basic system works reasonably well.

Be independent—throw away that straight axle: A straight axle may be a great piece of nostalgia. Proponents point out the simplicity and elegance of the basic design. Those points are all valid, but it won't hold a candle to a good independent suspension for ride or handling.

By separating the movement of one wheel from the movement of the other you create a system with dramatically improved ride. A bump encountered by one wheel doesn't move or affect the other wheel and this results in an improved ride.

Each wheel can now follow the road, wherever it might lead, independent of what the other wheel is doing. Each wheel is able to maintain much better contact with the asphalt and achieve better grip and overall better handling. If all that weren't enough, independent systems can be designed to provide anti-dive on braking and a nice low roll-center to improve handling.

But everything has its down side, and independent suspensions are no different. Compared to a straight axle, independent suspension systems are more complex and costly. Whether the high-tech

look of an independent system is good or bad depends on who's buying it and what type of car it is being installed on.

No matter which type of axle or suspension you decide to run, you will probably want to install an antiroll bar (sometimes called a sway bar). When you corner in your street rod, weight is transferred from the inside to the outside of the car and the car leans toward the outside of the turn. At best this is

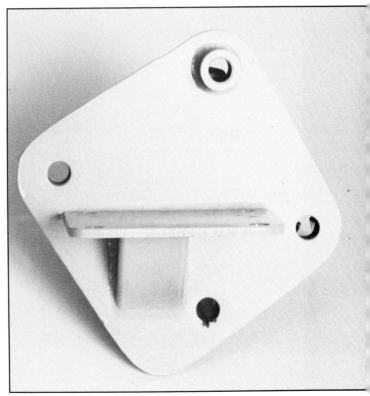

Bow tie fans can now mount a GM power or manual steering gear in cross-steer fashion on the rail of their 1937-39 Chevrolet with this mounting plate from Chassis Engineering. Chassis Engineering

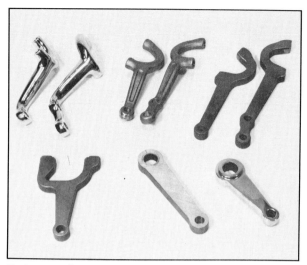

Each year there are more and more options for street rodders putting together a front suspension system. These steering arms and pitman arms from Posies are designed to solve a variety of installation and clearance problems. Posies

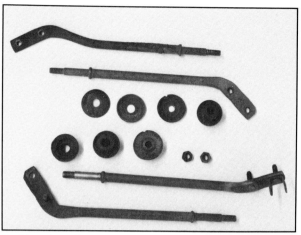

Rodders installing a Mustang II type front suspension should understand that strut rods come in a variety of shapes and sizes. Look around until you find the ones you need (though nearly any will have to be heated and bent). Be sure there isn't too much rust under the rubber bushings, and always replace those bushings when installing the front suspension.

annoying, at worst it can cause a loss of traction and control in the corner.

An antiroll bar is a means of resisting that weight transfer and preventing body roll. It has no effect, however, on vertical suspension movements where both wheels of an axle move equally. The bar is twisted only by unequal suspension movements and resists that unequal suspension movement by twisting or acting as a torsion bar.

The strength of the antiroll bar is determined by the actual strength of the torsion bar and the length of the levers that act on either end. How much antiroll bar you need is determined by the weight of the car (a bigger bar is commonly used at the front to control the additional weight at that end of the car), the type of suspension, and your personal tastes.

The Real World—Choosing a Suspension System for Your Car

Once you've decided which style of suspension is best for that new rod, you still have to go out and find the right one. Each year there are more and more systems to choose from and more and more decisions to make.

There are a couple of buying patterns that should be avoided. Don't buy a system based on sex appeal alone. Don't buy the system that looks best sitting on the stand at the Nats, hyped by the most persuasive salesperson.

You probably know what type of suspension you want. The next step is to find the manufacturer or components that offer the best quality at a reasonable price. Beware of systems that are claimed to "fit almost anything," especially if your street rod is an uncommon make or model. Try to find someone who can provide an unsolicited en-

dorsement of the system you want, mounted in a car like yours.

When buying a Mustang II style suspension, try to buy one that uses stock Ford geometry and a stock rack and pinion position. When the position of control arm pivots and the dimensions of the arms themselves are modified (to make them fit under early rods, for example) there can be too many surprises.

Buying an antiroll bar is pretty much a matter of checking the various catalogs to see what's available. Most of these bars are sold for a particular application. As usual, there is a formula for figuring the strength of a bar—suffice it to say that as the bar gets bigger, it gets stiffer. Remember too that the ends act as levers, and as the levers get longer the stiffness is diminished. So ask the dealer or manufacturer how stiff the bars are and if they were designed for a car with a big-block engine and A/C, or a small-block.

The other options are to adapt a bar from another car, or build your own antiroll bar. If you have to heat the bar to bend it, the bar will have to be heat treated again. You can scratch-build your own bar from 4130 chromoly for bars up to 1in diameter, or 4340 for bars bigger than 1in. After shaping the bar, take it in for heat treating and have it treated to 160,000 to 180,000psi (pounds per square inch).

Hands On—Installing the Front Suspension

We will track the installation of three different types and styles of front suspension. Those three are: a Boyd's independent system, a Heidt's independent system based on a Mustang II, and a straight axle with four-bars from Pete and Jake's. The idea is to give a good representation of the various systems that exist—and to cover the installation of the three

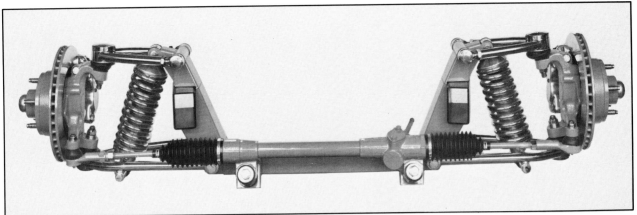

If you want more style than a Mustang II conversion, there are complete front suspensions available like this Superide II from Heidt's. This suspension features 11in rotors, tubular A-frames with threaded adjusters for caster and camber, and coil-over shock absorbers. Heidt's

most common styles of suspension used on modern street rods.

Boyd's Builds the Cadillac of Street Rod Suspensions

Street rods built at the Hot Rods by Boyd facility in Stanton, California, carry a very sophisticated independent front suspension. Available in either billet aluminum or tubular 4130 steel, these suspensions were developed with the help of Little John Buttera and borrow from race car technology of about fifteen years ago. First seen under cars like the Vern Luce Coupe (winner of the Slonaker Award in 1982), this system has evolved to represent the best in high-tech street rod suspensions. Owners of cars equipped with these systems like them for the way they work. The cars handle like a dream and continue to do so year after year.

The Boyd's independent system was one of the first that would fit correctly under the fenders of a Deuce and still look right when mounted to the front of a high-tech hiboy.

Though this system isn't available as a kit, installation instructions are included here for at least two reasons. One, it represents the techniques and procedures that you need to follow when installing some kind of one-off front suspension. Second, many of the steps outlined are the same ones that need to be followed for the installation of almost any front suspension.

The First Step—Getting Set Up

Before doing any suspension installation the frame must be correctly mounted at ride height in a jig or on a surface table. Comments made during the frame building chapter bear repeating:

"Constructing a quality frame that is straight and true requires a set of jigs, or more likely—a surface table. (This table can actually be a simple rectangular framework as described in the Frame chapter.) A surface table is just that, a table with a perfectly flat surface. Not to be confused with the

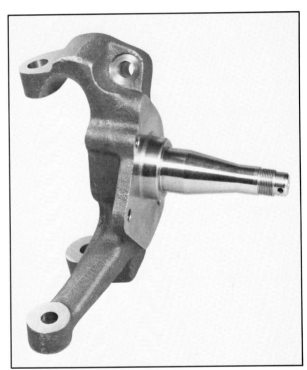

If your Mustang-equipped street rod just isn't low enough, you can always install dropped spindles like these from Heidt's and maintain full suspension travel and stock spring rate. Heidt's

floor of your garage, this table will allow you to set up two rails that are both at the same exact height. You won't have to wonder whether they are both at the same height because they were both measured from the table—the one that's flat and level."

Once you have the frame set up on a surface table or work area and you know exactly how far off the ground the rails are and that the "ground" reference is perfectly flat and level, you can begin measuring to determine where the front axle cen-

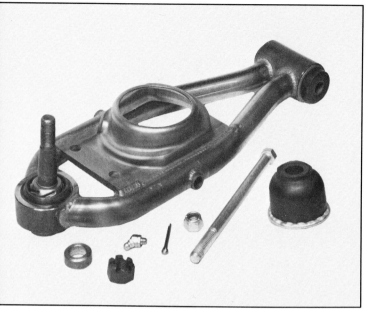

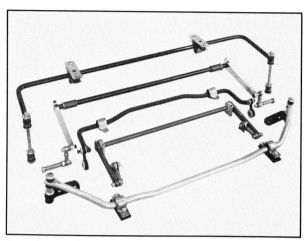

Sway bars and more sway bars. This selection from Heidt's is only a small fraction of the ready-to-install bars available for modern street rods on the market. The best advice as to how stiff they are and which one to run on your car comes from the manufacturer. Heidt's

Tubular lower control arms are available in place of the factory Mustang pieces. These arms come from Heidt's and feature ball joints and bushings already installed. Paint them or send them to the plating shop—or order them in polished stainless steel! Heidt's

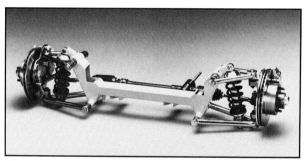

This complete independent front suspension from TCI features tubular A-frames (no strut rods), coil-over shocks, 11in ventilated disc brakes, and a 56in width. TCI

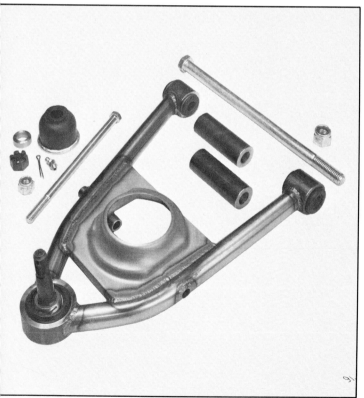

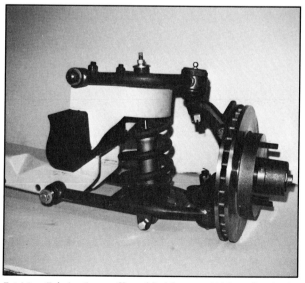

If you want to run a Mustang II front suspension or kit but don't like the looks of the strut rod, run these wide lower control arms and throw away the strut rods. These arms are from Heidt's and come with spacers and all necessary hardware. Heidt's

Fat Man Fabrications offers this Mustang II kit with tubular A-frames and a wide, low A-frame that eliminates the need for the factory strut. Fat Man Fabrications

This is what a complete chassis looks like "before." By laying everything out, Larry Sergejeff (or you) can do a good inventory before starting on the construction and fabrication.

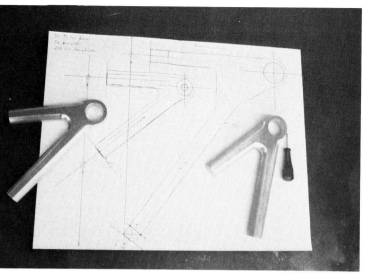

Many of the parts used on a Boyd independent front suspension are manufactured in-house. These upper A-frames were cut from 2024 T351 aluminum on CNC equipment.

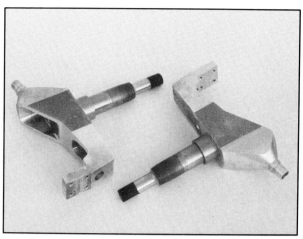

Spindle assemblies are made up of the heat-treated chromoly spindle pin, then press fit into an upright that is cut from more of the 2024 T351 aluminum. Steering arms will be bolted to the spindle upright. Bolt-on arms makes it easier to change the shape of the steering arm to suit different suspension setups or systems that run at different heights.

terline will go. You already know from your sketch how high off the ground the frame rails will be and (based on the diameter of the front tires) how far off the ground the spindles will be.

Step Two—Measuring

Once the frame is set up correctly you need to find the centerline for the front spindles. Larry Sergejeff at Boyd's always starts at the back of the frame and finds the centerline of the rear axle first. Next, he measures forward from the rear axle centerline, using the wheelbase for the car, and marks the centerline for the front spindles.

Of note here is that Larry and some other builders add 1/2in to 3/4in to the wheelbase of some fat-fendered cars in order to get the rear wheels far enough back in the fender opening. This is really a matter of taste and how low the car is going to be. There is no right or wrong, it's just one of those things to consider.

Based on that front axle centerline and the height of the spindles, the fixture that mounts the front spindles can be positioned and bolted to the surface table. Larry always marks the centerline of both the frame and the table. This measurement can be used to make sure that the spindles are mounted correctly side to side. Before bolting down the fixture, the axle centerline measurements should be double-checked and the crisscross measurement checked to be sure that the two axle centerlines really are parallel.

The Nitty-Gritty—Mounting the Components

Once the centerline and height of the spindles are known and the fixture mounting the spindles and

hubs is bolted to the table, the brackets for the A-frame pivots can be mounted to the frame.

Larry starts by correctly positioning the lower A-frame with the aid of brackets and clamps. The lower A-frame is mounted to be level in two dimensions.

The brackets that mount the A-frames are made from 3/16in chromoly plate. Larry prefers the chromoly for brackets as it is both stronger and also much tougher than mild steel. In an accident, the chromoly will withstand a severe overload. Chromoly is tough enough that if one of the suspension mounting bolts were to come loose, the bolt wouldn't "eat" the bracket.

Before cutting out any brackets, each pattern is checked to be sure the shape is correct. Once Larry has a good template or pattern, the shape is transferred to the chromoly, using a scribe to mark the pattern after the 4130 plate has been sprayed with machinist's blueing. After cutting, each bracket is checked to be sure it will fit the way Larry intended and then finish sanded to eliminate any rough areas.

Finally, the new bracket can be tack welded to the frame. First-time builders might want to tack weld everything together and then check all the dimensions and run the suspension through its full travel before doing the final welding.

Once the lower A-frame is in place, the upper A-frame can be positioned, again with the help of brackets and clamps. While the lower A-frame was set to be horizontal in two dimensions, the upper A-frame is mounted to be a little lower at the rear. The difference from horizontal is the same as the caster reading (more on caster in a minute). This puts the upper ball joint in the center of its travel and also

Before getting carried away with the installation of suspension components, it's a good idea to run a centerline down the frame. This can be used as a reference to check the correct placement of all components.

creates a suspension with some built-in anti-dive properties.

Though people on the street often say that both A-frames should be level as viewed from the front, the Boyd's system is designed to have the upper A-frame run downhill toward the center of the car. Whether the A-frames should be parallel or not depends on the total suspension design. (Beware of conversions of Detroit systems where the geometry has been modified—and what *were* parallel A-frames are no longer parallel.)

The upper A-frame must also be positioned to provide the correct caster reading. Though the camber and caster can be adjusted afterward, it only makes good sense to "manufacture" the suspension with everything set as close to perfect as possible.

In the case of the Boyd's spindle support, the caster reading can be read directly off the support. In most other systems it's pretty tough to measure the caster without turning the wheels back and forth through a 20deg arc each way.

Mounting the Steering Rack

Mounting the steering rack for the Boyd system is done by first finding a centerline that runs from the center of the hole in one steering arm and the hole in the other steering arm. Ideally, the centerline of the rack should run through this same line drawn from one steering arm centerline to the other. The rack itself should be mounted so that when the front wheels are pointing straight ahead, the rack is in the center of its travel and each tie rod is adjusted to exactly the same length.

Tie rod length is critical, not only in making the rack fit but in building a system with no bump-steer. Any changes that you make to the length of the tie rods must be done in conjunction with the length of the upper and lower A-frames and the position of the rack (see the illustration).

Once the rack bracket has been tack welded in place and the tie rod ends bolted to the steering arms, the front suspension is moved through its entire range of motion while monitoring the toe-in. Bump-steer is defined as a change in toe-in during up-and-down suspension movement. Small changes in toe-in that occur during suspension movement—bump-steer—can be fine-tuned out of the system by moving the rack up or down. When the suspension will move through its full range of movement with a minimal change in the toe-in, the bracket for the steering rack can be final welded to the frame.

Installing a Heidt's Mustang II Front Suspension

The front suspension "kit" illustrated here is a Mustang II style of suspension from Heidt's. The kit includes a cross-member, upper and lower arms,

Once the hubs are correctly located, the lower A-frames are attached to the frame with handmade brackets cut from 4130 chromoly.

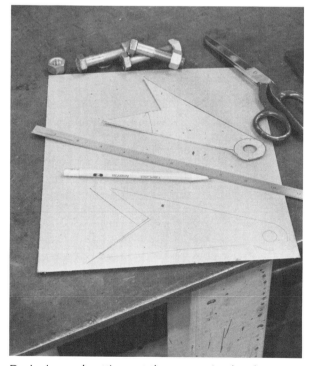

Designing and cutting out the suspension brackets must be done with the same care and precision used in the rest of the chassis project. Like most fabrication projects, this one starts with sketches, followed by the creation of accurate templates.

spindles, upper spring boxes, and struts for the lower suspension arm.

The first thing to do with any suspension installation is to get the frame correctly set up. Jim Petrykowski at Metal Fab in Minneapolis, works on a table—one that can be modified from one job to another. Readers might note the simple design of the table, the legs that bolt on and the height adjustment at the base of each leg. Jim is another builder who likes to work at ride height: "If you do all your work at the car's ride height then you have a reference, you know where the ground is, you know how the suspension is going to sit, you don't have to worry about lowering the car later because you know exactly how it's going to sit and everything is installed at that height."

The Setup

Jim starts by stripping the old suspension and the front cross-member out of the original '41 Ford frame. Next, the frame is mounted on the table and set up at ride height, according to the sketch that was done earlier. It is important to leave the front cross-member in the car or to tack weld in a cross-member at the very front of the frame before ripping out the old cross-member. This is done to keep the rails from spreading and twisting after the original cross-member is removed.

Next, the dimensions of the templates are carefully transferred to the 3/16in chromoly plate—the plate has been *sprayed with machinist's blueing to make it easier to scribe the design on the surface.*

Once the table is level and the frame has been set up at ride height you're almost ready to install the cross-member. Each manufacturer's kit is a little different and the instructions that come with the kits are sometimes a little vague. Jim likes to mark a centerline on the table (running the long way), matched to the centerline of the frame. This will make it easier to check the exact position of the cross-member, spring boxes, and control arms once they've been installed.

Before mounting the cross-member you also need to find the centerline of the front axle. Using the diagram that accompanies the kit, find your reference point and determine the front axle centerline. Fat-fendered Fords have a snubber hole on the bottom of the rails that marks the centerline of the front and rear axle. These snubber holes were used at the factory as locating holes to hold the frame while it moved down the line from one operation to the next. Otherwise, you can find the axle centerline by using the references shown on the instructions that accompany most of these suspension kits.

Once you have the centerline of the axle and the frame located you can install the front cross-member per the kit instructions. It's important to remember the old adage—measure twice, cut once. Be sure that the center of the frame matches the center of the cross-member. If you have any doubts as to the location of the cross-member, take the time to call the manufacturer and ask for a little technical advice; most manufacturers are happy to help. You might also want to ask the manufacturer if the centerline shown in their kit will put the wheel in the center of the wheelwell.

Mounting the upper spring boxes is the next step, one that should be done carefully. As Jim says: "A small difference of only 1/8in in the height of two spring boxes can cause the car to lean to one side. Also, if the spring boxes aren't mounted in the right position it will be impossible to set the caster and camber correctly." So be sure to mount the spring boxes per the instructions, and take care that they are the same height from the ground reference and the same distance from the frame's centerline.

As installed in original Pintos and Mustang IIs, this suspension put a little angle on the upper spring box, as viewed from the side. This angle builds a little

Larry cuts out the brackets on the band saw. If you don't have one of these sitting in your garage you can probably find a fabrication shop to do the cutting for you. A plasma cutter could be used here as well.

The partly finished brackets still need to be cleaned up and have the hole drilled.

A large cleanup sander smooths any rough edges and strips off the machinist's blueing. By clamping the bracket in a vise, a small hand-held sander could be used here just as well.

anti-dive into the suspension. Ask the manufacturer of your kit if the Ford-designed anti-dive feature will be left intact if everything is installed per the instructions.

(Some builders, when working with a new kit they haven't installed before, will tack weld on the upper spring boxes, then install the rest of the suspension, spindles, and hubs, and then do a quick and dirty check of caster and camber. In this way, if it takes all the available adjustment to get the car close to specs, the upper spring boxes can be moved slightly before final welding. The reason some street rods don't go down the road right is the poorly installed front suspensions that can't be aligned to factory specs.)

The lower control arms go in next, and once again there's plenty of room for error. If you (or someone else) installs new bushings at the pivot point for the control arm, they must be the correct bushings and they both must be pushed in the right way. This may sound obvious, but there are numerous replacement bushings out there in street rod

The finished brackets look great. Like the finished chassis, the key to quality is a good plan, carefully executed by individuals with enough skill, patience, and attention to detail to do the job right.

You can't assume the finished bracket will fit perfectly the first time. Larry does a trial fit (and a little more grinding) before finally tack welding the bracket in place.

Back to the frame, the lower A-frame is mounted so it is level in two dimensions. Though they aren't cheap, the electronic levels are extremely handy all through the process.

The upper A-frame is mounted next. Small brackets help to position the A-frames. Though the lower A-frame was installed to be level in two dimensions, the upper A-frame slopes downward toward the inside of the car, and slopes down two or three degrees toward the back of the car.

land, and at least two ways to put in each one. The goal is two lower control arms that sit in exactly the same position relative to the axle centerline. If the bushings aren't the same or if one was pushed in from the front while the other side was pushed in from the rear, then one will sit a little ahead of the other and the wheelbase will be slightly different from one side to the other.

After making sure the lower control arms have the correct bushings you can slide the control arms into place. Set each one on a prop or bracket of some kind so the bottom of the arm is roughly parallel to the table (these arms will end up parallel to the ground in most installations) and then measure each side, from a bolt hole in the control arm to the rear axle centerline or some known (and accurate) reference point. If there's a difference, it's probably due to mismatched bushings in the control arms. Again, beware of putting too much stock in the location of body mounting holes—a better reference point can usually be found.

Once the control arms are correctly installed, it's time to install the struts. Note that these struts come in a variety of shapes and configurations, so be sure yours are matched. The Pinto strut rods are shorter and often require less bending than a similar unit from a Mustang II. These struts often rust under the rubbers. If your struts are noticeably smaller in this area due to rust, replace them with new ones. Be sure to install new rubber mounting donuts; buy the

Here the level shows the front-to-rear angle of the upper A-frame. Larry installs the A-frame to have the same tilt as the caster reading. In this case the caster is +3.0 and the A-frame has a tilt of 2.8 degrees (lower at the rear).

The almost-finished front suspension. Upper A-frame is lower on the inside (this is part of the design of the suspension) and the rear mount is lower than the front (this provides some anti-dive and places the ball joint in the center of its travel).

These spindle uprights are designed so the caster can be read directly—in many cases the front wheels must be turned in each direction (with the use of a caster gauge) to get a caster reading.

later and "improved" versions or the heavy-duty version with the steel liner. Many of these bushings and the large washers are incorrectly installed, so note the illustration. Most of the time these struts (even the Pinto ones) will have to be heated and bent to work on a street rod.

You want to install the struts and end plates so there isn't a tremendous load on the control arm bushings when the installation is complete. A good installation sequence for the struts and end plates might go like this: Clamp the end plates in what you think is the right position on the bottom of the frame rail. Bend the arms and check the position of the end plates. After the arms have cooled, unclamp the end plates and install the struts to the end plates with new rubber bushings. Now, set the struts in place, bolt them to the control arms, and mark the frame for the final position of the end plates. Finally, disassemble everything and do the final welding of the end plates and the reinforcing plate.

Once the cross-member, spring boxes, and struts are installed, you can finish the job by installing the springs, spindles, and steering gear. When it's all done you can drive down the street (independently) in comfort, with a system that's light years ahead of a straight axle and available at a reasonable cost.

Larry holds the shock (without a spring) and its brackets up against the frame for a trial fit before tack welding the upper shock bracket in place.

Here all the brackets are tack welded to the frame. In the case of a first-time builder, it would be a good idea to run the suspension through its full range of movement before final welding. That is a good check to be sure everything is lined up as it should be. If possible, caster and camber should also be checked before final welding.

Installing a Straight Axle with Four-Bar Linkage

The four-bar and straight axle installation illustrated here is a system from Pete and Jake's utilizing a Bell tubular axle, a spring from Posies, and a variety of brackets, bolts, and miscellaneous bits and pieces. The four-bar and axle were installed on a Model A frame. There are a couple of things to note about this combination of components: First, the axle uses forged ends, a nice feature that ensures their durability and lessens the chance that the opening for the

At left

Small plates serve to strengthen and neaten each suspension mounting point. After all the angles and the suspension movement have been double-checked, the final welding can be performed.

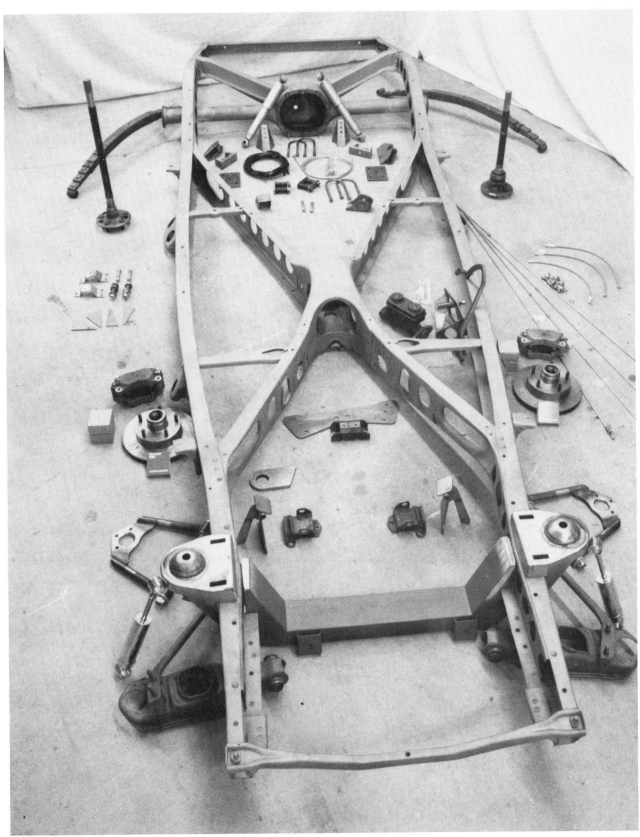

Another type of project—fatter and a little less high-tech. These are the parts needed to update a '41 Ford frame from stock to modern. The shop is Metal Fab in Minneapolis; the front suspension is Mustang II from Heidt's while the rear suspension is a leaf spring and shock kit from Posies.

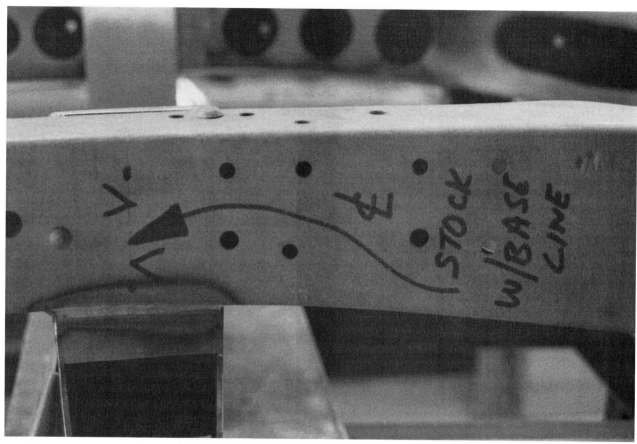

Like most suspension installations, the front axle centerline is a critical reference point and should be well marked and double-checked. Though this is a Heidt's kit, installation of most Mustang II kits is similar.

Location of the front cross-member depends on axle centerline and the centerline of the frame. In many of these cases, it's easier to weld everything with the frame inverted.

Once the cross-member is in place, it's a good idea to make sure the center of the cross-member matches the centerline of the frame. The centerline marked here will be used to check the position of the front suspension components.

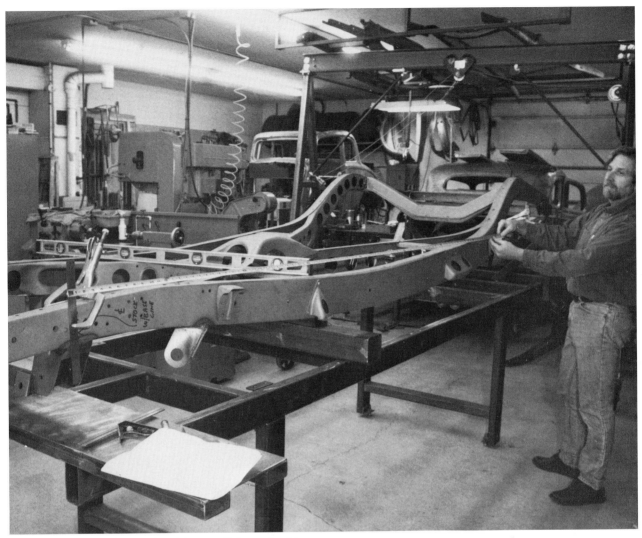

With the cross-member in place it's a good idea to double-check all the basic dimensions. Remember: Measure twice, cut once.

kingpins will elongate over time. Second, the spring perch is also a forged part—and these forged perches won't break off flush with the bottom of the axle the way some cast spring perches sometimes do.

Once again, the first step in this installation is the correct setup of the frame. Jim Petrykowski used jigs to mount the frame at ride height and then checked to make sure the frame was level side to side. Next, he marked the centerline of the table and then the centerline of the frame. Finding the centerline of the axle is easy with most Model A frames as the hole in the center of the front cross-member marks both the centerline of the frame and the centerline of the axle (it's still a good idea to check the centerline against another frame reference or the rear axle centerline).

The instructions that come with different brands of four-bar kits take slightly varied approaches to the

The location of the upper spring boxes is critical. Here, Jim Petrykowski of Metal Fab marks the position of the spring boxes on the stock Ford frame rail.

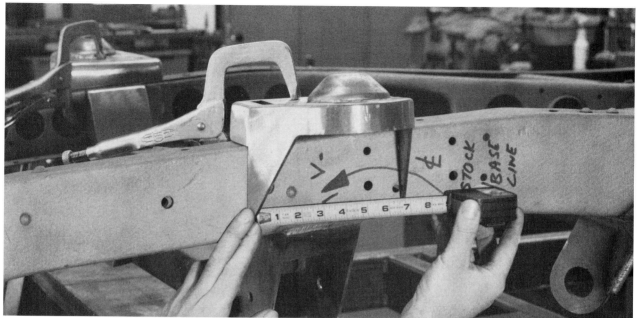

The spring boxes are clamped to the frame and then their position is carefully checked. A small error here can result in a car that leans to one side or one that can't be correctly aligned.

Jim spends considerable time checking the position of the spring boxes. Here he checks that each one is the same distance from the centerline.

The height of the spring boxes needs to match the dimensions supplied by the kit manufacturer. The best kits are those that retain stock Ford suspension locations and front end geometry.

In order to build a car that doesn't lean to one side, the height of the two spring boxes needs to be exactly the same.

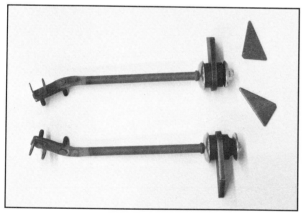

Strut rods usually need to be heated and bent to line up correctly with the edge of the street rod frame. These struts have been bent and new bushings have been installed (use heavy-duty bushings if possible). Install the bushings per the sketch in this book. The small triangular plates reinforce the strut mounting point.

At right
This is the Heidt's kit being installed. If you buy the bare kit and use junkyard components, be sure to replace all the wear items like ball joints and strut bushings. New bushings installed in the lower control arm need to be installed with care or the wheelbase will be different from one side to the other.

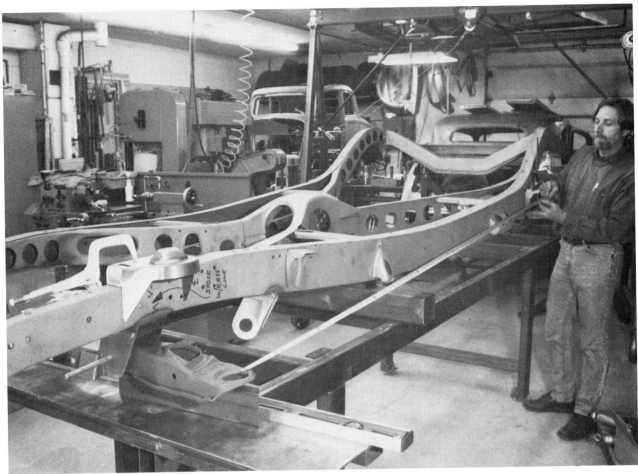

It's a good idea to temporarily install the lower control arms and then check dimensions again. This will reveal any error in the location of cross-member or in the way the lower control arm bushings were installed.

problem of correctly mounting the brackets. Some manufacturers give detailed drawings explaining where the brackets should be mounted, while others suggest that you hang the axle in the frame and then work backwards.

Jim chose to assemble the axle, the spring (with only one leaf), bat wings, and spring perch, hang the assembly from the front cross-member, and then determine where to mount the four-bar brackets. There are a few important things to remember, though, before getting too far along with a four-bar installation.

Because an axle suspended by a four-bar linkage moves back and forth slightly during suspension travel, it's important that all the linkage be set up and adjusted with the frame and suspension at ride height. If you adjust the bars with the suspension fully extended the bars will actually be a little too long—when the car comes down to ride height the axle is pushed too far forward, putting a bind on the spring.

Once the axle is hung from the spring and bolted into the cross-member, the bars can be installed and then the brackets can be clamped to

Here, the strut support is welded to the frame rail with the small reinforcing side plate. First-time builders may want to install the bushing kit on the strut rods and install the struts in the lower control arm—and then mark the location of the strut rod support.

49

Everything has been temporarily installed before final welding to check geometry and positions. It's a good idea to mock up the entire kit like this and then check both the wheelbase and the alignment.

This is what the spring box looks like after final welding. Note the concave section formed to provide clearance for the spring.

This is what it looks like after final welding. Note that the frame has been partly boxed just behind the cross- *member (with small discs of steel that come with the kit) and welded along the top seam.*

the frame. In order to do a really neat installation, Jim has a few hints: "If you pre-assemble the bars on the bench, you can get each one to the same length and be sure the two ends are parallel. I usually leave three or four threads showing on each rod-end." It's a good idea to take a little extra time to make sure the brackets mount neat, level, and even from side to side. In particular, just because the top of the frame is level doesn't mean the bottom is—especially if yours is an original frame.

Use a carpenter's square to make sure the brackets are square and that the bolt centerlines are parallel to the ground. By carefully measuring each side against a frame reference point you can be sure that the two brackets are mounted correctly and that each is in the same position on the frame rail. Before tack welding the brackets in place, check them

At right
Ready for suspension components, the '41 Ford frame is set up for a small-block Chevy engine and TH350 transmission.

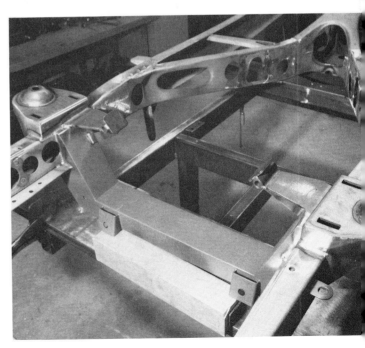

Wheel Alignment:
Understanding the Basics

Understanding which suspension to buy and how best to install it is much easier if you understand wheel alignment and the various alignment angles. Understanding wheel alignment is really a matter of understanding three angles: caster, camber, and toe-in. Here is an overview of the three:

Camber: Camber is the inward or outward tilt of the wheel at the top. Measured in degrees, camber is the tilt of the wheel from true vertical. If the wheel tilts out at the top, the camber is positive; if the wheel tilts in toward the car at the top, the camber is negative. The idea is to keep the tire planted flat on the road for maximum traction and grip. Sometimes a car will require something other than 0deg (zero) camber while at rest in order to achieve good grip and tire wear while the car is going down the road.

Caster: Caster is the backward or forward tilt of the spindle support arm at the top. It is a directional control angle measured in degrees, the amount that the centerline of the spindle support arm (or kingpin) is tilted from true vertical. The best example of caster is the front wheel of a bicycle. The fork tilts back at the top, providing quite a bit of positive caster and a great deal of directional stability to the bike. If the fork were vertical (zero caster), riding "no-hands" would be almost impossible.

Toe-in: Toe-in or toe-out is the difference between a measurement taken across the front of the tires and one taken at the same spot on the back of the tires. The actual toe-in is seldom zero. A setting of $1/16$in or $1/32$in is common—and done so when the car is rolling down the road and resistance puts a load on all the steering and suspension pivots, the two wheels are running parallel to one another.

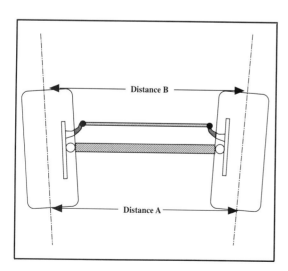

The camber angle is simply the tire's tilt from vertical as seen from the front or rear. Positive camber is a tilt to the outside, negative is a tilt to the inside.

At left
Toe-in is the distance between distance B and distance A. Don't use the grooves in the tires when checking toe-in. Instead, mark the tread with a scribe as the tire spins (car on a jack). The best idea is to have the toe set on a professional front end alignment rack after the car is finished.

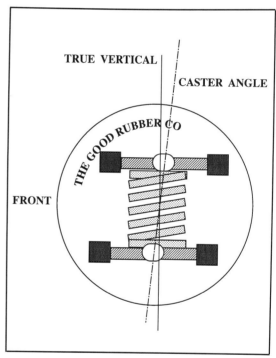

Caster is more easily understood if you think of the front fork of a bicycle. Like a bicycle fork, the king pin, or ball joints, of a car are usually arranged so the centerline of the turning axis meets the road surface out ahead of the tire contact patch. Most cars run positive caster, as shown here, a situation that provides good straight-line stability.

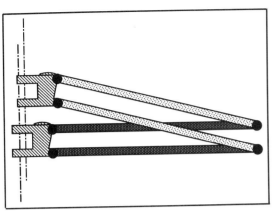

As a four-bar system encounters a bump, the axle is free to move up without any caster change or any twist being placed on the axle. Note that the axle does move back slightly as it moves up.

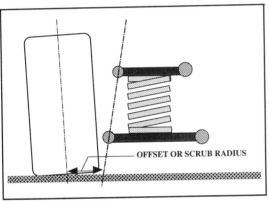

OFFSET OR SCRUB RADIUS

Scrub radius is the distance from the tire centerline to the centerline of the king pin or ball joints. All front suspensions are designed with a particular scrub radius dimension. When you add wheels with more or less offset from those that came with the suspension, you change the scrub radius.

As long as we've gotten this far into the discussion of front suspension geometry, there are a few more things to consider:

Wheel offset: Wheel offset is not an alignment angle at all but is a very important part of the overall handling and suspension picture nonetheless. If you draw a line through the kingpin or ball joints (front view) and then another line through the center of the tire, the distance between those two lines (where they intersect the ground) is called offset, or scrub radius (see the illustration to avoid confusion). Designers of modern cars sometimes brag that they have achieved zero scrub radius, meaning that the two lines intersect where they meet the ground.

No matter what the actual measurement is, when you change the wheel and wheel offset on the front of your car, you effectively change the scrub radius. More wheel offset means more scrub radius, which also means that now the wheel has a lot more leverage to act on the rest of the steering linkage. Changes in wheel offset from what the engineers intended will have profound effects on vehicle stability, brake performance on uneven surfaces, and a driver's feel for the road.

Ackerman effect: One more thing to consider before leaving the subject of alignment is the Ackerman effect, or toe-out on turns. Think of the front wheels of a car as the vehicle makes a turn. The Ackerman effect is the degree by which the inner front tire turns more sharply than the outer tire in a turn. In order to keep the car turning around a common center (and keep in mind that the inner tire runs on a smaller diameter circle), the inner tire must turn more sharply than the outer tire. If the outer tire is turning 20deg from straight ahead, the inner tire usually turns 22 or 23deg (check the illustration again). This effect is essential to good handling and is created by the angle of the steering arms. The bottom line is the importance of correct steering arm shape and the sometimes frightening effects that come from rearranging the steering arm angles or location of the steering gear.

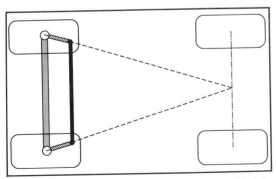

Ackerman Effect, part 1: Part of the reasoning behind the Ackerman Effect can be seen by looking at a car from above. The centerline of the two steering arms meets near the differential, the angle of the steering arms produces toe-out in turns.

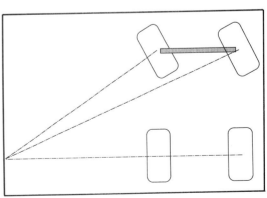

Ackerman Effect, part 2: In a turn, the inside tire turns a little more sharply than the outside tire. Thus, all the tires rotate around a common center point.

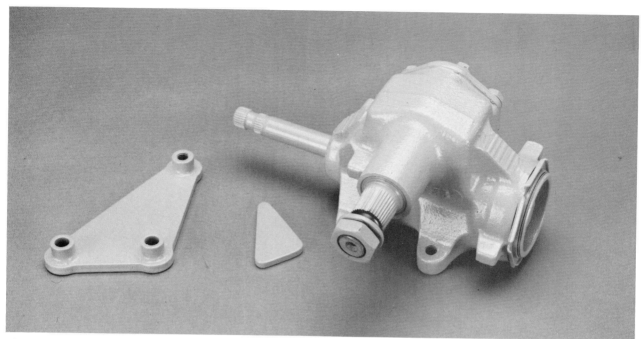

This new GM 525 gear with mounting plate is from TCI and offers a good alternative to the dwindling supply of Vega gears. TCI

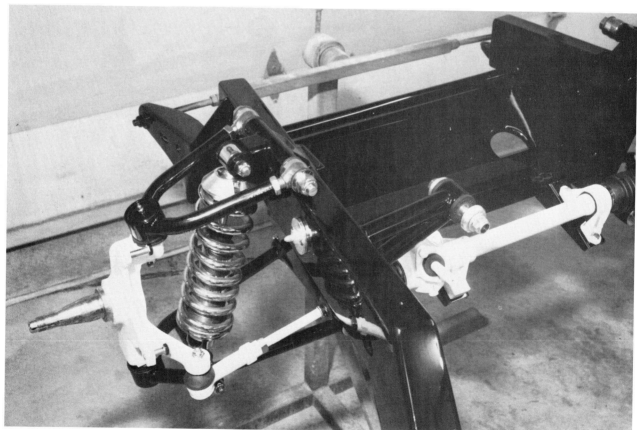

This is Gene Younk's 1939 Buick chassis with a Heidt's Superide system—tubular A-frames, coil-overs, and a rack and pinion mounted in rear-steer fashion.

This unusual and innovative suspension seen on the front of a Model A roadster features torsion bars mounted in the frame rails and air shocks that provide height adjustment.

against the frame centerline. Jim Petrykowski always stresses the fact that "Those brackets have to be correctly positioned in three planes. Too often people only think in terms of one or two planes."

Once the brackets have been tack welded to the frame, it's a good idea to double-check all the dimensions and the position of the front axle. Is the wheelbase correct, is the front axle positioned correctly in terms of both its centerline and the centerline of the frame? The idea is to get everything set up correctly without using the threaded adjustments on the bars. It just makes for a neater installation. Leave the threaded adjustments for the final adjustments done at the alignment shop when the car is all finished.

Before the final welding, use a protractor or electronic measuring gauge to check both camber and caster. Camber can be checked right off the wheel hub, caster can be checked by using the flat area on top of most kingpins and correcting the reading by 90deg (it's necessary that both the axle and frame be positioned at ride height to check caster and camber).

After the caster has been checked (and the axle is in its final position), it's probably a good time to mount the front shock absorber brackets. You probably want to run the suspension through its full movement so the shocks end up with two-thirds of the travel left for compression and one-third for rebound. Remember to keep the two mounts as close to parallel as you can.

If you want something unusual, then just whittle out your own components from billet aluminum.

Most of us can't design and fabricate a complete front suspension, but the persistent rodder can "borrow" exist- ing geometry and then have the pieces carved in any style he or she chooses.

After checking and double-checking all the dimensions, you can finally weld up the four-bar brackets. The frame should be boxed, at least in the area where the brackets mount, and the welding should be done by a skilled welder.

When properly installed, the new four-bar installation will ride easy because there's no bind on the spring or the linkage. It will be easy to align because it was set up correctly the first time. And anyone who looks it over will have to admit, "Damn, that's really a nice installation," because you took the time to plan everything out and do a neat job.

Theory—Steering

Steering Design Options

There are three typical styles of steering linkage used in most street rod applications: cross-steer, drag link, and rack and pinion. The three basic layouts go like this:

Cross-steer: Cross-steer systems use a gear mounted on the left frame rail and a long drag link running to the right side steering arm. The system as generally installed with a straight axle is simple, easy to install, and keeps the pitman arm and drag link neatly out of sight. Correctly installed, this system offers good steering control and minimal bump-steer. Disadvantages include clearance problems if the starter is on the left side or the drag link is too close to the oil pan.

Drag link: Drag link style steering utilizes a long drag link running on the outside of the left frame rail, as seen in some older rods and many Bucket-Ts. The system avoids most of the clearance problems seen in cross-steer systems. The down side includes a tendency to bump-steer and a need to be very cautious with the specific layout for the sake of correct geometry. (See the illustrations.)

Rack and pinion: A rack and pinion system has the advantage of precision steering, good road feel, and ready availability. Properly installed, a rack and pinion system has a reputation for zero bump and roll steer. If the front suspension is an independent Mustang system or a Mustang clone, a Mustang rack and pinion is the only logical answer. The proverbial downside includes two major obstacles: first, the near impossibility of using a rack and pinion with a straight axle; second, the difficulty in correctly mounting a rack and pinion to any front suspension unless that suspension was designed for the specific rack and pinion gear.

Speaking of innovative street rodders, the system seen here was designed by Jim Prokop who fabricated, or had fabricated, nearly all of the suspension components.

Even the sway bar was bent up specially and then heat-treated. Note the adjustable sway bar link.

The difference between work that is only OK and work that is really nice is in the details. This isn't high-tech, it is just a good design and very neat execution. Each of these little brackets was fabricated by hand.

Jim's suspension features upper and lower control arms and an adjustable torsion bar. You probably don't want to try to duplicate a suspension for yourself unless you have a good engineering background and a lot of patience.

The torsion bars on Jim Prokop's car (a Dodge Brothers touring rig) are adjustable at the rear mount. The frame— already pretty sturdy—has been reinforced on the inside of the channel in the area of the rear torsion bar mount.

The power steering rack is adapted from a Volvo (the suspension is in full droop here), mounted to brackets on the frame cross-member.

This is the four-bar kit that Jim Petrykowski installed in the Model A. The axle is from Bell, the steering gear is a rebuilt Vega gear from Mullins, and the spring perches are made from forged steel.

The simple table at Metal Fab is put into service again. The front frame bracket is a simple device bolted to the frame horns and clamped to the table.

Possible Geometry Problems

Installing the front suspension and steering linkage so as to avoid any bump-steer requires a little thought. It's easy to overlook a potential problem and build a system with incorrect geometry.

The possible geometry problem is best illustrated by looking at a drag link system. Bump-steer in this system occurs when the bump causes the axle to move forward or backward more than the drag link. The effect varies depending on the style of axle mounting (see the illustrations again), but the end result is the same. Basically, the axle and the end of the drag link that attaches to the axle must move through the same arcs (or nearly the same) as the suspension moves up and down over lumps and bumps.

If the gear being mounted is for a cross-steer application the geometry problem still raises its ugly head, though the actual problem is axle movement to the side rather than to the front or rear. The gear itself, be it a Vega manual or General Motors power unit, should be mounted so the pitman arm is pointing straight ahead when the gear is in the center of its movement. It is also important that the gear be mounted so the drag link is parallel to the tie rod.

With a cross-steer system, any axle movement to the side during suspension travel will effectively

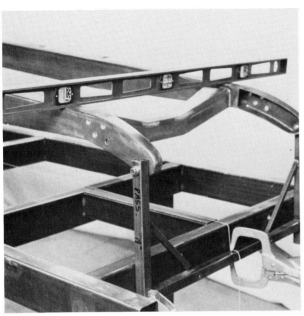

The frame needs to be set at ride height and must be level from side to side.

Though the axle centerline is easily found on a Model A (it's marked by the hole in the front cross-member), Jim Petrykowski double-checks the centerline against the holes in the frame horns. The centerline has been marked on both the table and the frame rail.

It's not a bad idea to check the centerline against another reference point farther back on the frame.

'32 FORD
4-BAR FRONT END KIT

SPECIAL NOTE: For best results frame should be boxed from front crossmember to firewall. If this is not possible, frame must be boxed at least in 4-bar bracket mounting area.

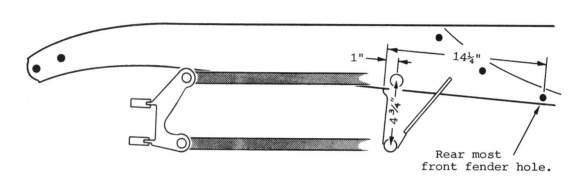

1"   14¼"

4¾"

Rear most
front fender hole.

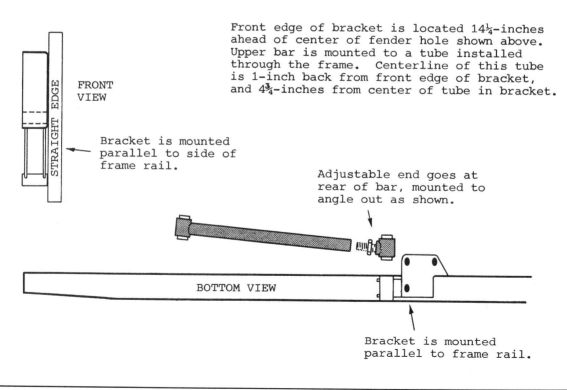

Front edge of bracket is located 14¼-inches ahead of center of fender hole shown above. Upper bar is mounted to a tube installed through the frame. Centerline of this tube is 1-inch back from front edge of bracket, and 4¾-inches from center of tube in bracket.

FRONT
VIEW

STRAIGHT EDGE

Bracket is mounted
parallel to side of
frame rail.

Adjustable end goes at
rear of bar, mounted to
angle out as shown.

BOTTOM VIEW

Bracket is mounted
parallel to frame rail.

Good suspension kits come with good installation instructions. Pete and Jake's offers good installation tips with their kits. Here is a sample page from one set of instructions accompanying a four-bar kit.

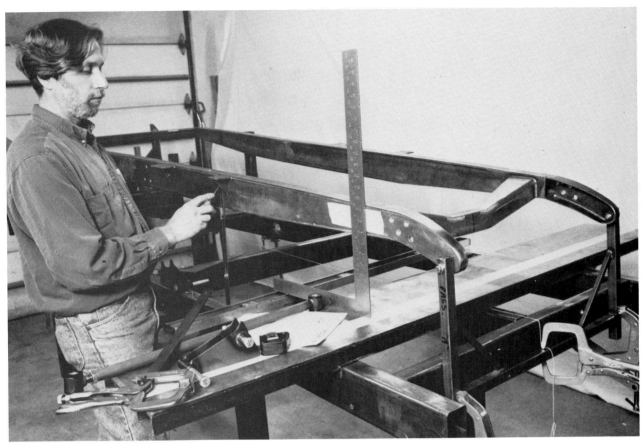

The Pete and Jake's directions show the location for the four-bar brackets (not all kits do), so Jim marks the frame with the preferred bracket location so he can check and see how the brackets line up later.

change the length of the drag link and create the dreaded bump-steer problem. Street rods with a leaf spring, mounted buggy style with a shackle at either end, have the capacity to allow lateral axle movement on the shackles.

We've all seen street rods with buggy style springs and cross-steer linkage—and no panhard rod. Yet, most street rod equipment manufacturers recommend a panhard rod in these applications. The panhard rod prevents side-to-side axle movement, though the rod itself (see the illustration) must be mounted very carefully so as not to create more problems than it solves. If in doubt as to the need for a panhard, consult the manufacturer of your components.

While pondering all these linkage variables a builder should also consider the steering ratio and the effect that the pitman arm length has on that ratio. In general, a longer pitman arm will provide faster steering—a given amount of steering wheel movement will result in more drag link movement. With manual steering and a big V-8 a very fast ratio will mean "armstrong" steering. A variety of arms are available for the most popular gears and provide some fine tuning of the turning ratio, geometry, and final gear position.

To keep the installation very neat, Jim assembles the four-bars so each has the same number of threads (about four) showing. He also makes sure the two ends are perfectly parallel.

Jim Petrykowski and his dad pre-assemble the axle using only the main leaf. This axle uses forged ends, a nice feature. The spring perches are forged steel as well. The axle comes with instructions that warn the user to be careful if the axle is chrome plated for fear of causing hydrogen embrittlement. If you have one of these chrome plated, be sure the plating shop knows how to avoid the embrittlement problem.

This is what it looks like with the axle and four-bars hung in place. Spacers were put under the axle to get it to ride height.

A cautious builder would be wise to mount the steering gear and linkage temporarily, until he or she is sure: the ratio is correct, there are no clearance problems, and the gear lines up as intended with the steering column.

Buying Components

The Vega steering gear has become the manual gear of choice for most modern street rods using cross-steer installations. It has the advantage of being inexpensive, compact, and easy to find. Pitman arms of different shapes (often needed to clear oil pans and such) and lengths are readily available.

If the gear you buy is a bone-yard refugee, be sure it is adjusted correctly before installation. Most *Motors* and *Chilton* manuals contain a good section on adjusting a manual steering gear. If in doubt, rebuilt gears are available from a variety of street rod sources.

Lately it seems the Vega gears are becoming harder to find. After all, they haven't made any Vegas for several years now. The GM manual gear, often called the 525 gear, is just a little larger and is often used instead of the Vega gear.

As the street rods we drive (and in some cases the street *rodders*) get larger and heavier, there is more and more demand for power steering. If you choose to install a complete Mustang II type suspension, then the gear usually comes with the kit, and a factory power rack and pinion is an option. These Ford power racks can usually be connected to a late-

A variety of references will be used to ensure that the axle is correctly mounted in the frame. Here a plumb bob is dropped through the kingpin hole to check the axle centerline.

The axle location is checked against the rear axle centerline to make sure the wheelbase is correct.

Take nothing for granted. Here we check that the axle is centered in the frame. It's a good idea to do a quick check of the camber and caster about now, using a protractor or electronic level.

model GM power steering pump without any hassles except the minor problem of getting the hoses sized correctly. Otherwise the pressure and valving are compatible between the Ford rack and the GM pump.

If you've chosen to stay with a straight axle design, you can still have power steering. Many of the mounting plates for GM steering gears will allow you to bolt on either a manual or a power steering gear. The biggest problem with the power steering gear is the extra room it takes up on the left side of the engine. Fat Fords from 1935 to 1948 will generally accept a power steering gear, though clearance is tight. In most situations, you need to run a specific manifold on the left side (in one case, a Chevy truck manifold is needed) or certain brands of headers. As with the manual gears, a variety of pitman arms are available to make a good installation as easy as possible. More information on which power steering gears work in which cars with which exhausts can be found by contacting the manufacturers of the mounting plates and suspension systems.

The drag link running from the gear to the right side steering arm is usually available as a kit, or it can be fabricated by a good street rod shop. The drag link must have some adjustment for length in order to get the steering wheel centered correctly while keeping the gear in the center of its movement (more later). The right side steering arm with double female ends necessary to attach both the drag link and the tie rod, is available for most popular spindles as well.

Always mount the upper shock bracket after the caster has been checked. That's so you don't mount the upper bracket and then change the angle of the lower shock bracket when the tilt of the axle is adjusted.

Be careful in your choice of steering arms and tie rod ends. The tapered end of these tie rod ends isn't always the same, and a tie rod end mismatched with the wrong female end in a steering arm can draw up too far or loosen up later. Be sure the male and female tapers are all the same.

Consider, too, the comments made in the wheel alignment sidebar in this chapter about the Ackerman effect. That "toe-out on turns" is created by the shape of the steering arms. Heating and bending the steering arms to clear a wishbone should only be done by experienced builders. As the selection of new steering arms continues to grow it seems more likely that you can just buy the steering arm you need—designed for your combination of axle, frame, and suspension—rather than being forced to modify an existing arm.

Hands-On—Steering

The general guidelines for mounting the steering gear include the necessity for rigidness—you want all the steering wheel motion translated into wheel motion. If the frame or steering mount flexes, that flex will be transmitted to you as lost movement and sloppy steering. Just as important as rigidness is the necessity for correct geometry.

You probably want to clamp the gear mounting bracket (available from a variety of sources) in place and then mock up your linkage and possibly the column as well before doing any final welding.

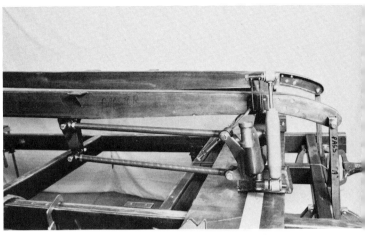

A side view of our new four-bar suspension. It would be a good idea to spend a little time making sure the four-bar brackets are perpendicular to the ground, at the same height, the same distance from the center of the frame, and the same distance from the axle centerline.

When you're mocking up the gear and linkage, place the gear in the exact center of its movement, point the wheels straight ahead, and center the steering wheel. This will put the gear in the center of its travel when you're going straight down the highway. An adjustable drag link will allow you to precisely center the steering wheel and keep the gear in the center of its travel.

Getting the gear in the center of its travel is important for a number of reasons—the biggest

Once the four-bars and axle are correctly mounted, it's time to mock up the steering gear and linkage.

67

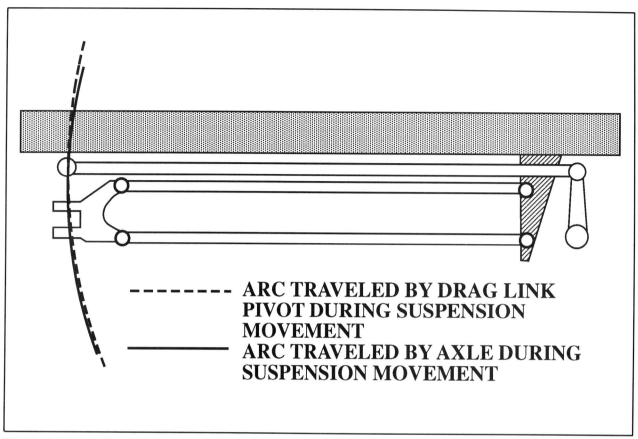

**ARC TRAVELED BY DRAG LINK
PIVOT DURING SUSPENSION
MOVEMENT**

**ARC TRAVELED BY AXLE DURING
SUSPENSION MOVEMENT**

With a four-bar style of front suspension, the drag link should be kept parallel to the four-bars. By mounting the link in this fashion, the arc traveled by the axle and that traveled by the end of the drag link are nearly identical. Remember, the axis is only moving through 3-4in of travel.

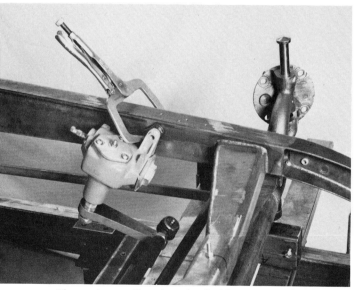

The neat mounting plates for the Vega gears make it easy to mount the gear to the side of the frame rail. The gear should mount so the drag link is parallel to the tie rod. The gear must be mounted so the worm shaft (the one that runs up toward the column) clears the motor mount and the exhaust.

being that most gears have a "high-spot" in the center of their travel intended to compensate for wear that might occur in the straight-ahead position.

Many street rods are built with the steering gear mounted so the worm gear is parallel to the frame rail. This is usually done to put the pitman shaft perpendicular to the ground and make sure the pitman arm moves back and forth without any up-and-down movement. While this arrangement may make it easier to clear the oil pan with the drag link, it makes for a more complicated shaft from the steering wheel to the gear. How you mount the steering gear is up to you, but understand that you don't have to mount it so the worm shaft is parallel to the frame rail. Detroit "points" the worm shaft at the column in order to avoid a complicated shaft with three U-joints, and you can too.

No matter how you mount the gear, be sure there's sufficient room between the oil pan and the drag link when the suspension is bottomed out and try to keep the drag link parallel to the tie rod.

The gear mounting plate (whether this is a cross-steer or drag link application) should be mounted to a boxed frame rail. When you finally bolt that gear to

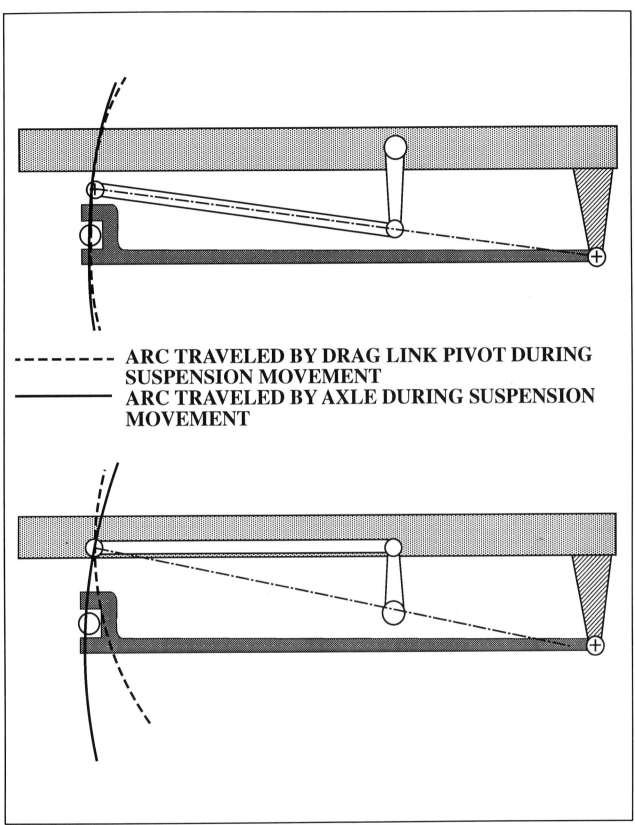

- - - - - - ARC TRAVELED BY DRAG LINK PIVOT DURING SUSPENSION MOVEMENT

——————— ARC TRAVELED BY AXLE DURING SUSPENSION MOVEMENT

In a drag link style of steering linkage, it's important that the drag link centerline run along the line from the wishbone pivot and the drag link attachment point. Failure to design and mount the linkage correctly will result in bump steer. Note the lower illustration and the large difference in the arc traveled by the axle and that traveled by the end of the drag link. Simply "keeping all the linkage parallel" isn't good enough.

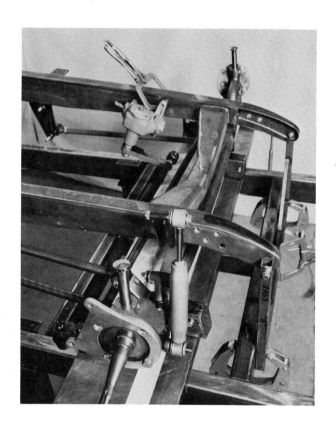

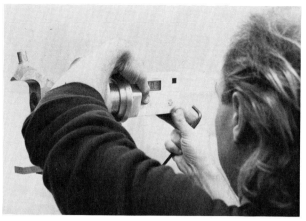

Larry Sergejeff uses an electronic level to check the camber of a hub in the fixture. A simple protractor could have been used too.

At left
The steering gear can be mounted at an angle as shown— which makes for a less complex shaft from the column to the gear. Make sure the drag link and pitman arm will clear the oil pan. It would be a good idea to set the motor and transmission in the frame before you settle on the exact location for the steering gear.

Here the motor mounts are set in place with a fixture to check their location and any interference with the steering gear.

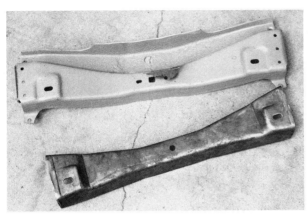

Two Model A front cross-members. The upper one is an original, the lower is a modern replacement. The center hole marks both the frame and the axle centerline.

the mounting plate, use grade eight bolts and a little Loctite. As stated before, any movement in the mounting plate will translate into sloppy, vague steering.

If you decide to install a panhard rod, the rod should be parallel to the drag link and of the same length—so it moves through the same arcs as the drag link and you encounter no bump-steer.

When you've mocked-up everything, spend a little time running the new gear lock to lock with the suspension bottomed out and fully extended. Watch for clearance problems at the oil pan and the exhaust. Starting in the center of gear travel (and the wheels pointing straight ahead) make sure that "full lock" is the same number of turns in each direction. After spending hours on the creeper checking clearance and movement, it's finally time to weld in that steering mounting plate.

Finishing Up—Mounting the Column and Shaft

In choosing a column, many street rodders buy a late-model GM unit. While certainly not the only game in town, most GM columns have some kind of slip fit, extendable shaft. This means that adjustments in length can be accomplished by disassembly, shortening or lengthening the center shaft, and then sectioning the outer column case. It's not as hard as you might think and should be kept in mind if you can't find just the right column.

In mounting the column there are a few basic rules of the road and some common misconceptions to avoid: first, the column should be mounted to provide a good angle between the column shaft and the steering gear. Second, and often overlooked, the column should be mounted to provide a comfortable driving position. With the possible exception of Bucket-Ts, the lower column should pass through the firewall high enough that it doesn't interfere with the placement of your feet or your foot movement from the gas to the brake pedal.

Third, the mounts used to attach the column don't have to be 1/4in boiler plate. Plate in the 3/32in to

Another Vega gear, this is a rebuilt unit available from Pete and Jake's.

These little numbers are caster shims, used to tilt the angle of a straight axle in a twin leaf spring situation. These were purchased at a truck alignment and frame shop and can also be used to adjust the pinion angle in a leaf spring car.

Installing the steering rack on the '33 Ford frame at Boyd's starts by marking the centerline of the rack. The ruler runs from the center of one steering arm hole to the other—and marks the centerline of the rack and pinion gear.

Using the ruler as a guide, Larry gets ready to tack weld the rack and pinion mounting plate to the frame. The gear needs to be installed so it's in the center of its travel when the wheels are pointing straight ahead.

Larry makes sure the rack is in the center of its movement and that each tie rod is the same length.

Still a very popular choice for a cross-steer application with manual steering, the Vega boxes are compact and there are a number of different pitman arms available to solve any clearance problems.

Here the rack is mocked up in the frame. This rack is a Fiat unit. Design of the rack and length of the tie rods must be coordinated with the rest of the suspension design and dimensions. You can't just adapt a rack and pinion to another suspension without doing a lot of homework first.

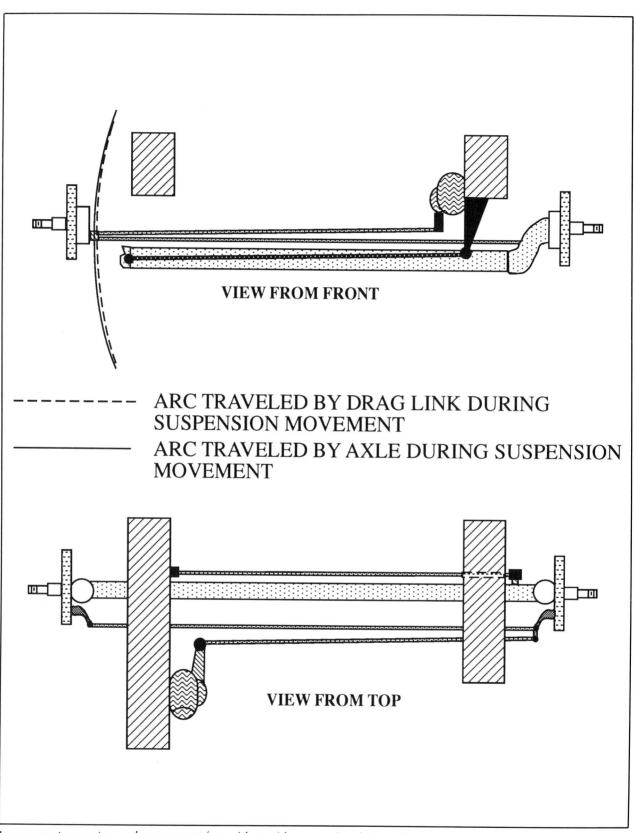

VIEW FROM FRONT

- - - - - - - - - ARC TRAVELED BY DRAG LINK DURING SUSPENSION MOVEMENT

———————— ARC TRAVELED BY AXLE DURING SUSPENSION MOVEMENT

VIEW FROM TOP

In a cross steer system, axle movement from side to side will cause bump steer and lack of steering precision. To prevent this type of movement, a panhard rod is often used. Builders should keep the panhard rod parallel to the drag link and keep the length of the two rods the same. This will help avoid dreaded bump steer. Note that when the system is well designed, the two arcs are nearly identical.

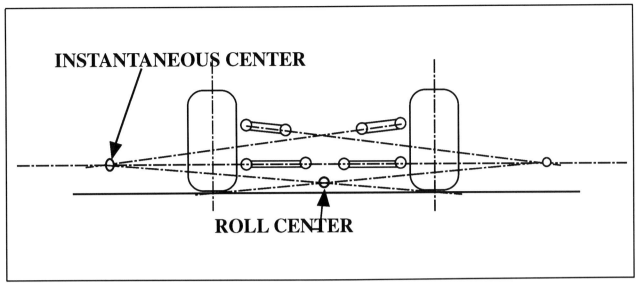

This illustration is intended to show how all the parts and dimensions of the front suspension contribute to the total design. Anything you do, from a change in tire diameter to a change in spring height, will affect something else. Thus it's always better to build it right the first time rather than building it and then making a series of changes. It's also better to stay with the factory dimensions and geometry when using complete sub-assemblies from other cars.

3/16in range is certainly adequate. Fourth, the column must be mounted at both ends (some dashboards may need reinforcement). If there is a case for overkill on the mount it's on the lower, not the upper, column mount.

Like the steering gear, the column should be mounted temporarily until you are sure the angle and mounting will work out perfectly.

Get the Shaft

Some kind of a flexible coupling is needed between the steering column and the steering gear. Detroit usually uses one or two U-joints and a "rag" joint. The rag joint is used to isolate road noise and to compensate for any shifting between the body (mounted on some kind of cushion mounts) and the frame.

Any U-joints you use should be needle-bearing U-joints. Joints without needle bearings are often available, but are intended for industrial or racing applications. Always use a good needle-bearing U-joint, either a quality aftermarket joint or the OEM (original equipment manufacturers) joint, and nothing else. U-joints should be kept in their working range, usually less than 30deg, and when more than one joint is used they must be kept in phase.

When laying out the column/gear/frame relationship remember that the best systems are the simple ones. Remember, too, that while the steering gear must be mounted for correct geometry there is usually some flexibility in the final position. Finally, remember that exhaust systems can usually be moved or modified—don't go to a lot of work designing a complicated shaft with three joints just to get around an exhaust pipe.

There you have it: a steering gear mounted for correct geometry and a column mounted for good driver position and comfort.

Chapter 4

Rear Suspension

Introduction

This chapter discusses the various rear suspension systems available for your car. Like the front suspension, there are numerous systems and styles of suspension available for the rear of your street rod, with more coming on the market every year. The discussion includes a short comparison of the various suspension designs and some guidance for the day you have to choose among all those systems and brands to actually take one home.

The hands-on section documents the installation of the three most popular styles of rear suspension: A Boyd-built independent system based on a Corvette system, a simple leaf spring installation in a fat-fendered Ford, and a four-bar installation in a Model A.

Theory

Like front suspension systems, rear suspension systems are available in a number of different styles. The possibilities range from a relatively simple solid axle with leaf springs to a fully independent system with custom billet hubs and inboard brakes.

The criteria you use in determining which system is best will be the same used in deciding which front suspension to use: money, sex appeal, handling, and style. If your budget forces you to compromise, it's probably best to spend more

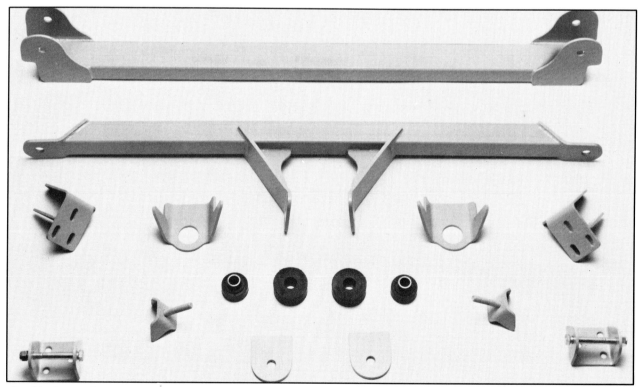

This kit from Chassis Engineering adapts the pre-1984 Corvette rear suspension to a '33 or '34 Ford chassis. The kit uses all Corvette parts, including the trailing arm, outer carriers, shocks, brakes and spring. Chassis Engineering

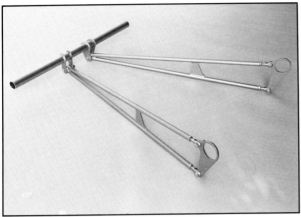

This Model A ladder bar kit from Pete and Jake's is designed to fit original or reproduction Model A frames. It features urethane bushings at the front and adjustable clevises at the rear. Pete and Jake's

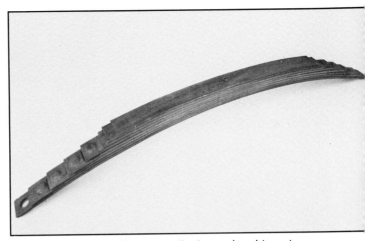

The company known for springs, Posies, makes this spring for street rods running the Corvette independent rear suspension. Posies

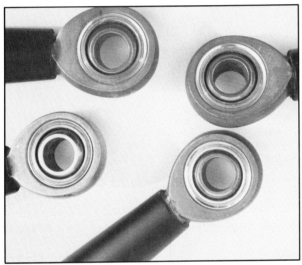

Heim joints like these are often used at the ends of a suspension member or link. Though they're expensive, true Heim joints are nearly indestructible even in severe duty, and never need lubrication.

Designed to work in conjunction with the Posies spring, these adjustable spring-perch bolts are intended for street rods running Corvette suspension. Posies

money on the front suspension. Those are the wheels that steer the car and that, in most cases, carry the majority of the weight.

Suspension Design—Which is Best

In the broadest sense, there are two kinds of rear suspension, independent and solid. Nearly all the solid axle designs can be divided by the type of spring: leaf or coil. Coil spring systems can be further divided according to the design of the suspension system. The coil spring suspension systems most commonly seen on street rods are parallel 4-bar, triangulated 4-bar, 3-bar, and ladder bars.

A discussion of the various rear suspension systems and the highs and lows of each would have to start with the most simple and progress to the complex.

Leaf springs: Perhaps the best buy for the money is plain old leaf springs supporting a nice used 9in Ford or 10-bolt GM rear end. Leaf springs are readily available, inexpensive, and require low maintenance. Leaf springs do a good job of distributing any weight bias on one side of the car and are capable of handling a lot of torque. Because the leaf springs locate the axle as well as support the car, these systems do not require a panhard bar. Finally, a leaf spring rear suspension generally gives reasonably good handling and ride.

Every design has its flaws, and leaf springs have theirs. The downside to this design is the "stiction" that occurs between the leaves, the lack of adjust-

This is a good look at a simple ladder bar installation in an early Ford frame. Good ladder bars are long. These reach nearly all the way to the transmission mount.

More and more street rodders are running sway bars on both the front and rear of their cars. The strength of the sway bar is determined by both the bar's diameter and the length of the "lever" on each end.

ability, and the minimal sex appeal of a leaf spring rear suspension. Some of these problems have been addressed by the street rod industry. Posies makes their Super Slide springs with little Teflon buttons separating the leaves and minimizing internal friction (Teflon liners are also available). Chrome leaves are available (or you can have your own chrome plated) to increase the visual appeal, but you still end up with a system that is tough to adjust.

Getting a leaf spring suspension lower can be done with the good old lowering blocks. Some people pull a leaf out of the spring-pack, though this is considered a no-no by most people because the spring-pack was designed to work as a package. The best solution is to have the springs de-arched, a process that can be performed by most large spring companies.

Coil spring suspension systems: Coil spring systems offer a number of advantages as compared to leaf springs, and just a few disadvantages. Coil spring systems are more easily adjusted, due to the ease of swapping springs and the adjustment collar on most street rod coil-over assemblies. Coil spring systems are generally considered to have good sex appeal and some of the designs do a good job of

Ladder bars require a panhard rod to prevent lateral movement. This panhard rod will be nearly level when the car is at ride height, and is well supported on both ends.

Another Corvette system, kind of a Boyd-style system mounted under a '33 Ford with components carved from billet. Note the struts—a good way to keep the system at ride height during assembly.

Another sway bar, this one fabricated by Jim Prokop and then heat treated. Note the neat lower mounting bracket integrated into the axle saddle.

providing traction if yours is a serious go-fast kind of project.

The downside includes the need for a panhard rod (in most systems) and the increased cost if you are converting an early rod from the original leaf springs to a coil spring system.

There are at least three separate types of coil spring rear suspension systems available—four-link (also known as a four-bar), three-bar and ladder bars. A discussion of coil spring rear suspensions starts with the most popular, the four-bar system.

Four-bar rear suspension: Four-bar rear suspension comes in two versions, parallel and triangulated. Parallel systems run two pairs of parallel rods forward from the rear-end housing to the brackets on the frame. In most applications the coil-over mounts behind the axle. The parallel rods locate the rear end housing fore and aft, allowing it to move up and down (much like the system used on the front of many cars). A panhard rod is used to locate the rear end laterally. This rod absorbs side thrust and prevents excessive side-to-side movement of the rear end relative to the frame.

The parallel four-bar system has the advantage of being readily available from a variety of sources. Most kits include coil-over shock units reasonably

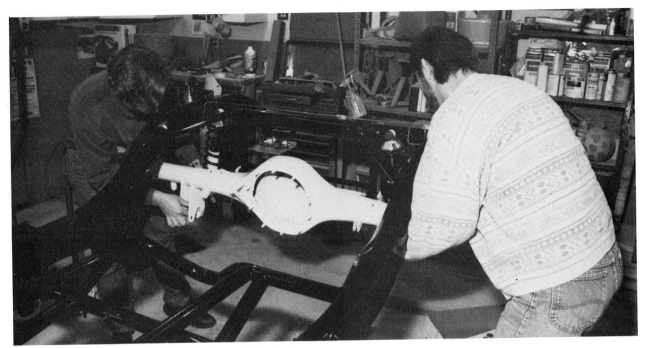

This is Gene Younk's Buick chassis, as he and Jim Prokup assemble the three-bar rear suspension.

well matched to the popular cars. The system offers good ride, good handling, and easy adjustability. The downside to this design includes the need for a panhard rod (more linkage to mount).

The other type of four-bar system is the triangulated four-bar linkage. This system uses two rods running forward from the rear-end housing to brackets on the side rails of the frame—these rods run parallel to the side rails. The other two rods run from the rear end housing to the frame at an angle relative to the frame rails. When viewed from above, these rods form a triangle. Because they run at an angle compared to the other two, they absorb side thrust and eliminate the need for a panhard rod. Some builders don't feel these systems handle hard corners as well as a pure four-bar and complain further that it's hard to run the exhaust with the upper triangulated bars in the way.

An interesting alternative to the more common four-bar systems is the three-bar system. Though seldom seen on street rods, the three-bar has been around a long time and is often used on certain drag race applications.

Like a triangulated four-bar without the two top triangulated bars, a three-bar uses two long, parallel bars and one shorter top bar. This systems uses a panhard rod to absorb side loads. The major advantage is simplicity and traction. The downside is the lack of a kit (to the best of my knowledge), meaning you have to build your own or have one built by a shop like Boyd's or Metal Fab.

The simplest of the coil spring systems is ladder bars. Like a simplified four-bar, the ladder bars mount

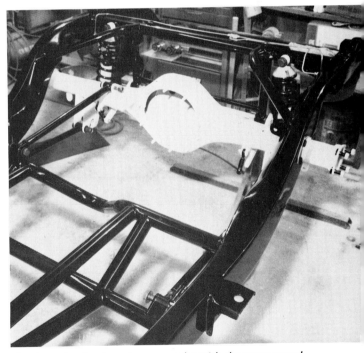

The three-bar has long been popular with drag racers and some fabrication shops. This three-bar installation and X-member fabrication was done by Metal Fab. Note the two long lower bars and the third shorter upper link.

to the rear-end housing and to a common point on the side rail of the frame. Ladder bars are simple, adjustable, and available from a number of suppliers. They transmit power directly to the frame, at a point

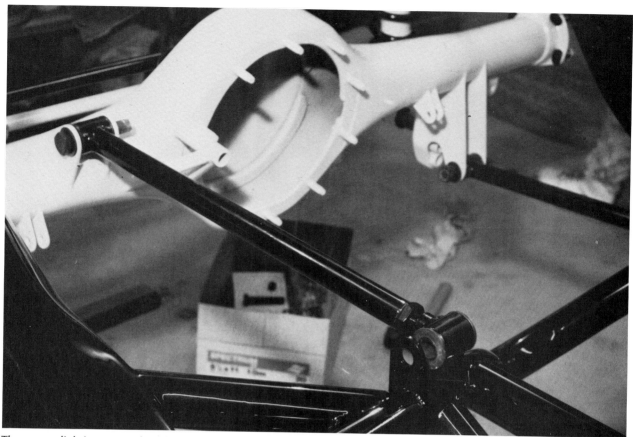

The upper link is mounted under compression until the suspension has some weight on it. The mount for the panhard rod can be seen on the Ford 9in rear-end housing.

Sway bars can be mounted on the top or bottom of the rear end, depending on the situation.

well forward on the frame. Ladder bars usually help give a car a good launch and are popular with drag racers.

Ladder bar systems do require a panhard rod, however, and don't seem to offer the visual appeal of a nice chrome four-bar system. Because the bar mounts to a single front pivot, there is also considerable change in pinion angle as the suspension moves up and down. The amount of pinion angle change depends on the length of the ladder bars—longer is better. Street rodders (with the emphasis on the word *street*) complain that ladder bars don't corner as well as some other systems and that again, the bars make it hard to route the exhaust.

If nothing but the best will do for your street rod, then of course there is only one rear suspension system to consider—the fully independent rear suspension. Advantages include better handling and ride but what the independent really has all over any other system can be described in two words—*sex appeal.*

Independent rear suspensions: If you want your car to be the one people get down on their hands and knees to look under, then slide a modified Corvette system under it with polished axles and inboard brakes. The downside includes cost, com-

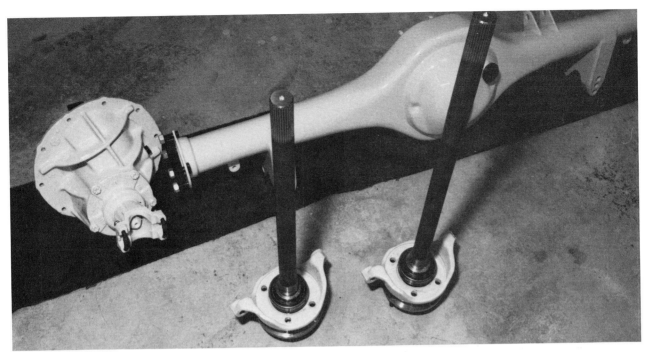

Gene's Buick runs the hard-to-find Ford 9in rear end from the Lincoln Versailles with factory disc brakes.

Another frame at Boyd's shop. The frame and rear end are both set at ride height before the rear suspension is installed.

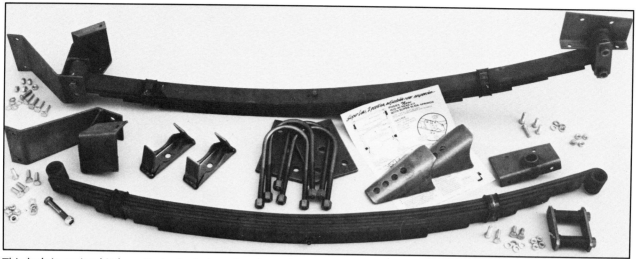

This bolt in spring kit from Posies is designed to fit Fords from 1932-48 (different years take a different part number) *using nearly any rear axle housing and is two-position adjustable. Posies*

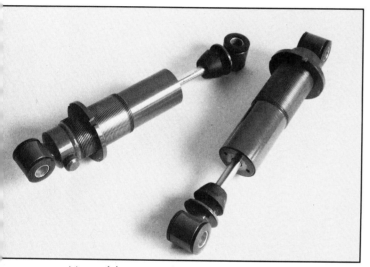

Many of the suspension systems seen under modern street rods use coil-over shocks like these. The rubber bushing on the shaft is not intended to function as the suspension stop.

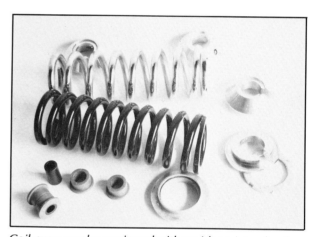

Coil-overs can be equipped with a wide variety of springs in many different ratings and styles.

plexity, maintenance, and the limited choices available when it comes to buying a kit. But if money is no object and you've got to have the best, then this is the only system to have.

The Real World—Choosing a Suspension System for Your Car

As already mentioned, the big advantage of a leaf spring rear suspension is the relatively low cost and the wide availability of parts. Not only junk yard parts for the scroungers out there, but brand-new springs designed for early Ford and Chevy rods from companies like Posies, Chassis Engineering, Speedway Motors, and a dozen more. Before you buy, look for a manufacturer who's been on the scene for a number of years. Be sure the kit is really designed for

your car and not designed to fit "almost any Ford of any year." Ask if the springs are de-arched and if there is any provision for height adjustment.

Buying a four-bar system is tougher because first, you need to decide whether to buy a parallel or triangulated system. Purists point out the fact that a parallel system offers more near perfect geometry while a triangulated system has the links moving in different planes. Jim Petrykowski made the comment that "with a triangulated system, when you corner real hard the rear end seems to break away without any warning."

If your rod will run "in the weeds" with only a few inches of suspension travel, then it may not make any difference.

When you buy the four-bar system for your car, be sure it is designed for your car. Look for extra holes and mounting options so you can mount it in the position you need and get the ride height where you want it. People have been known to build their

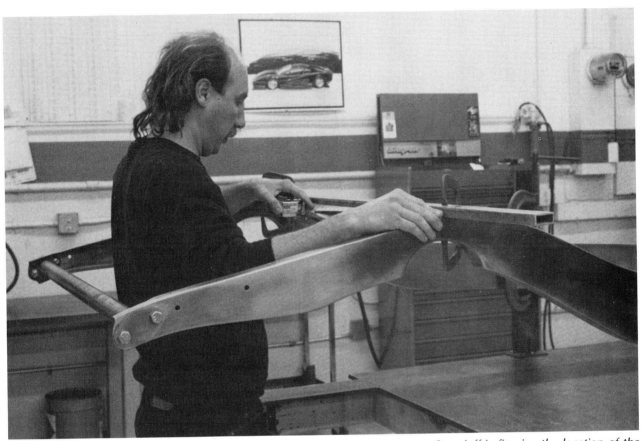

This same frame has been seen in past chapters, and it is now ready for independent "pussy-footing" rear suspension. First things first; the square tubing marks the axle centerline. Larry Sergejeff is figuring the location of the mounting plate for the Corvette center section.

The center section will be supported by a network of tubing. The rails have been "C-ed" for extra clearance and are fully boxed. Chassis is set at ride height for all the installation work.

Using a few shims, the mounting plate for the center section is clamped in place and checked to be sure it is level. The mounting plate location is determined based on the axle centerline, tire diameter, frame centerline, and desired pinion angle. Pinion angle on this frame is close to zero (the engine runs downhill one or two degrees from level).

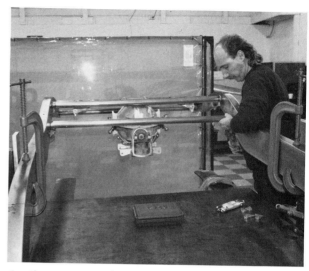

Another cross-member at the front helps to absorb torque and transfer it to the chassis. Like the X-member, these cross-members are made from mild steel tubing, 0.120in thick.

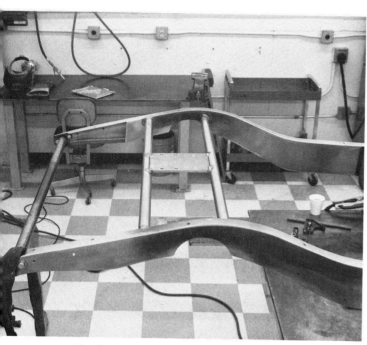

After both main cross-members are welded in, the mounting plate will be checked again to be sure it is level in both dimensions.

Cross braces are used to further support the center section and also serve as the mounting point for the upper shock absorber mount.

own four-bar systems. That's fine, just be sure the bars are long enough to provide good geometry and that all the components and rod ends are strong enough for the task at hand. The panhard rod, too, should be as long as is practical. A longer rod means that as the suspension moves up and down, the body will experience less side-to-side movement. A too-short panhard rod might move the body enough in certain situations to cause the tire to rub on a fender lip.

Buyers of ladder bar kits should keep in mind the same points made for other coil spring systems: buy from a well-known manufacturer, and longer ladder bars (and panhard rods) are better than short ones. Look for lots of adjustability in the brackets.

No matter what kind of rear suspension you buy, ask the manufacturer where their kit places the tire in the fender well (front to rear) when everything is installed according to their instructions. The factory wheelbase often needs to be lengthened slightly in order to get the rear tires centered under the fender.

Independent systems offer less choice than the other systems as there are fewer manufacturers of kits and fewer shops that regularly tackle these jobs. Most of these systems are based on either a Corvette or a Jaguar rear suspension. Those in the know report that the Corvette is a much more durable unit and parts are generally easier to get (though there seem to be some new Jaguar systems coming out as we go to press).

The Corvette suspension comes in two basic designs, the early design offered on 1963 through 1983 Corvettes and that used on 1984 and later Corvettes. A change was made in the housing in 1980, and those in the know say that the earlier, cast-iron housings are stronger and that a greater number

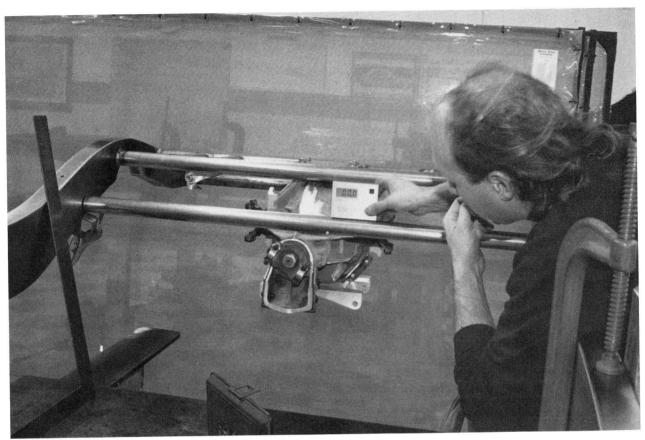

Once again, the small electronic level is used to check the position of a chassis member.

A look from underneath. Brackets and the center section rear cover have been cut from billet aluminum. Brackets on the side to the housing will mount the inboard brake calipers. Note the upper shock mounting point.

A look at the Corvette center section and cover used in this installation. The center section is the aluminum housing used on Corvettes from 1980-83. Some builders prefer the earlier (1963-79) cast-iron housing because the cast iron is stronger than aluminum and there are more gear ratios available for the cast-iron housing.

Further along, the forward cross-member has been welded in, as have the short struts that support the front of the center section housing.

Once the center section is mounted, it's time to hang the axles and hubs on the car. Normally the disc brake rotors would be mounted by now, but the rotors didn't arrive in time for the photo session.

A fixture is used to mount the hub assemblies on either side. The hub-to-hub distance is 56in on this and many Boyd-built cars. Hub-to-hub dimensions must be figured during the planning phase and coordinated with the choice of wheel offset.

As with the front suspension members, the rear hubs and linkage are available in either 4130 chromoly or aluminum.

At left
Like the front suspension members, the aluminum hubs for the Boyd-built rear suspension system are cut in-house from heat-treated aluminum billet on a CNC machine.

Here Larry hangs a plumb bob to show the axle centerline. Hub position is determined by axle centerline, hub-to-hub distance, and wheel diameter. It's always a good idea to check the distance from each hub to the frame centerline.

The rear hub is mounted to be parallel across the bottom. Lower linkage arm runs roughly parallel to the ground.

A close-up showing how the plumb bob marks the axle centerline. Hubs are positioned so the axles run downhill toward the outside by about two degrees at ride height.

Upper link runs forward from the hub. Position of upper link is determined by the hub design.

Rear view of the almost-completed rear suspension. Everything's installed except the springs and the inboard mounted brakes.

of ratios are available for the earlier housing. The best known of the Corvette-based rear suspension systems comes from Hot Rods by Boyd. First used in the early 1980s, these systems have evolved into an ideal street rod suspension. As offered in kit form, the system comes with its own subframe and all the components necessary to mount it between the rails of your street rod. Included are tapered axles, inboard disc brakes, and aluminum hubs.

If you are the really independent type, then kits are available from Chassis Engineering as well as other manufacturers to allow the mounting of the Corvette system into most early street rods.

Hands-On

Installing the Boyd's 'Pussy-Footing' Independent Rear Suspension

The independent rear suspension developed by Boyd and his craftsmen is known as the "Pussy-footing" rear suspension. It is based on the pre-1984 Corvette rear suspension and generally uses the aluminum center section seen in 1980-83 Corvettes. Though usually seen only in the complete cars and chassis to come out of Boyd's shop, this unit is available as a bolt-in kit to fit most street rods.

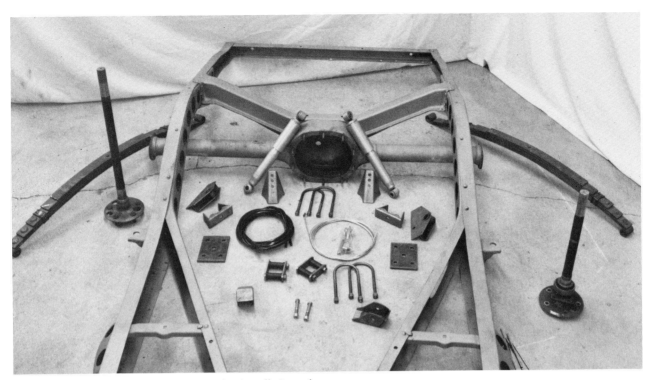

The "before" shot of our next project, the installation of two new leaf springs and a Ford rear end in a '41 Ford frame at Metal Fab in Minneapolis.

As always, the installation starts by locating and marking the axle centerline. Fat Ford frames have an axle snubber hole on the bottom of the frame rail that can be used as a centerline reference.

A Discourse on the 9in Ford Rear End—and a Few Alternatives

Why the 9in Ford?

So you're building a new street rod and you wonder if in fact the venerable 9in Ford rear end is the best one for the job.

The 9in Ford rear end is very popular and the reasons are simple: It's strong, parts are readily available (both new and used), it's relatively easy to narrow, and it uses the "pumpkin" design with a removable center section.

The 9in Ford gets its strength both from a strong housing and good stout gears, with good contact between those gears. The Ford housing (there are different models available) is generally stronger than either the 8³/₄in Mopar or the 12-bolt GM housings.

Finding a 9in isn't too tough as the design was used for thirty years. The first 9in Ford rear ends were used in passenger cars and trucks as far back as 1957. Though the passenger cars used the 9in only until 1973, the pickup trucks used them until 1984, and full-size Ford vans used the 9in right up through 1987.

Narrowing the Ford rear end (a necessity in most street rod applications) is easier than some others, as the tapered section just behind the axle splines is short. In the case of the Mopar 8³/₄in rear end, the axle tapers to a smaller diameter behind the splines—and the smaller diameter section runs almost halfway up the axle shaft. This means that when you cut the end off the axle to make it shorter, the diameter of the shaft where you cut it isn't large enough to spline. So if you want to narrow a 8³/₄in Mopar rear end, plan to buy two new axles.

The design of the third-member style rear end (a design feature shared with the Mopar and the smaller 8in Ford) means that you can drop out the center section—for work or maintenance or to install another center section with a different ratio—in a matter of an hour instead of a full day.

If there is a downside to the 9in Ford design it might include the price and the availability of used positraction units. Though thousands and thousands of these rear ends were manufactured, demand by street rodders, drag racers, off-roaders, and anyone else interested in a really tough rear end means that prices aren't always cheap. If you want positraction with your rear end, the availability goes down and the price of course goes up.

How to Tell a 9in from a 9in

The Ford 9in was offered in a variety of housings and with a variety of axle and bearing combinations. First, beware of imitations. Ford manufactured a 9³/₈in rear end, visually quite similar to the 9in. The trouble is there are few parts available for this oddball rear end. You know the rear end is the larger model if you can place a socket straight onto the housing stud at the 7 o'clock position. The other visual difference is the top, horizontal rib on the housing. If the rib turns sharply down at one end, it's the 9³/₈in rear end. (Note: A clever shop can easily modify the larger housing to accept a 9in center section.)

The 9in housings were offered in two basic styles with one variant. More than ninety percent of the housings seen at swap meets have a single vertical rib at the top of the housing. A few are the stronger, two-rib design that was used during the first few years of production. Rarely you will see a nodular housing, made from extremely strong nodular iron. These nodular housings feature a large N, cast into the housing itself.

Ford manufactured 9in rear ends with different axle diameters, different axle spline counts, and different size wheel bearings. It's a little confusing but it goes like this: Axles came in 28- and 31-spline versions, in two shaft diameters. The larger diameter axle uses a larger wheel bearing. Thus the larger axle/bearing combination is not interchangeable with small diameter/small bearing housings. A 31-spline axle is always the larger diameter shaft but a

The Ford 9in rear end has been popular for years with the high-performance set. Here we see a narrowed and reinforced housing, a nodular-steel center section (note the large N in the casting), some Strange axles (from Strange Engineering) and a spool for full-time two-wheel drive.

On the left is a two-rib 9in center section, used during the early years of production. On the right, a similar but smaller 8in Ford center section.

The strongest factory axles are the thirty-one spline design (seen on the left). Besides having more splines than the twenty-eight (on the right), they also have a larger diameter for stronger engagement.

Ford axles for the 9in come in two diameters and use a variety of bearings. These axles are both large diameter. On the right is the most common bearing style, the tapered roller. The other bearing is one of a number of sealed styles that were used by Ford or are available as a replacement bearing.

28-spline axle can be either the large- or small-diameter axle shaft.

Large-diameter axle shafts with the larger bearings have an axle housing inside diameter (ID)—at the wheel end—of 3.150in. Small diameter axles with smaller bearings (the smaller diameter axles are always 28 splines) have a housing ID of 2.89in. The 31-spline design is thirty-five percent stronger (torsionally) than a 28-spline shaft cut on the same diameter axle. The added strength comes from the larger diameter at the spline and the increased number of splines.

Besides the two different sizes of axle bearings, there are different styles of bearings as well. One of the most common is the tapered roller bearing. This bearing is lubricated by rear-end lube and features a seal on the outside of the bearing. New bearings of this style are easy to find and purchase. Special sealed bearings that will replace the tapered roller bearing are also available. Single- and double-row ball bearings were used by the factory as well. Some of these are sealed bearings and use a separate seal

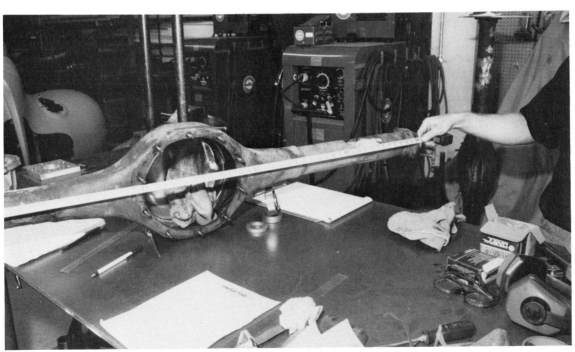

Before starting to cut that rear-end housing, you need to know exactly how much to take off each side. How much you remove must be coordinated with your wheel and tire selections.

continued on next page

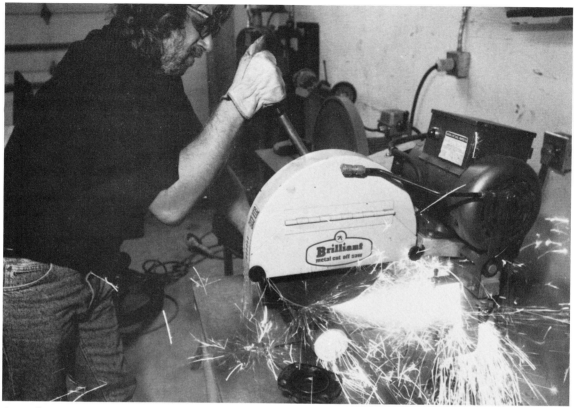

A cut-off saw is used to shorten up the housing.

on the inside of the axle. Some trucks with 31-spline axles used a special double-row ball bearing that is unique in size and expensive to replace.

Summers Brothers, a manufacturer of special axles and components for many types of rear ends, makes a special wheel bearing that will allow you to run the large-diameter Ford axles in a housing built for the smaller diameter bearings and axles.

Which One is for You?

Trying to decide which style of 9in to look for is mostly a process of elimination. The narrowest of the 9in housings were used in some Ford Granada models. Some of these (and the Lincoln Versailles) also had factory disc brakes, a nice touch. If you can find the Granada housing (a large *if*) it will probably be narrow enough for some later street rods (most of these measured 61 or 62in from flange to flange. For most of us though, the 9in you buy from the boneyard will have to be narrowed.

If you can't find the narrow Granada-Lincoln model, buy the widest 9in housing you can find. Buy one from a pickup truck or large passenger car. This way you are more likely to get a large, heavy housing and axles that are both large in diameter and long. Remember, there's a tapered area behind the splines with a smaller diameter. You want an axle with enough extra length that when you cut it, you cut off

all of the tapered section. The larger diameter axle will already be 31 splines, or at least big enough that it can be resplined from 28 to 31 splines.

Positraction for the 9in

Like the rear ends themselves, a variety of what we call "posi" units were offered for the Ford 9in design. The Equa-Loc and Traction-Loc are similar in design. Both were offered in two- and four-pinion designs, with four-pinions being harder to find and much stronger. Both designs use clutch discs to control differential action. The Traction-Loc is the better of the two designs and is available in both 28 and 31 splines. The Equa-Loc is available only for 28 spline axles.

More durable and more expensive is the Detroit Locker. This is a true locking differential with both wheels positively driven whenever the car is moving straight down the road.

A third option is available for full-time drag cars. This is the spool. In essence, the spool eliminates the spider gears and provides a locked rear end—all the time. Cheaper than even a used Equa-Loc, a spool or mini-spool can help the racer on a budget ensure that both tires receive equal power.

Making It Narrow

Before you can have that rear end narrowed, there is the problem of measuring how narrow to

continued on next page

The axle flange isn't just butt-welded back on. Instead, a lathe is used to cut a step in the flange end of the housing.

A fixture like this one keeps the flanges in line when the ends are welded back onto the housing. It's easy to warp a housing, so weld the flanges back on last, and do it with a fixture like this one.

make it. There are two ways to do this. The easiest way is to put the tires you intend to run on the rims you intend to use. With the car on jack stands at ride height, carefully locate the tires where you want them to be. Once the tires are correctly located, raise and lower the car to ensure there is room for fender lips and suspension components.

As a rule of thumb, there should be at least 1in of clearance between the tire sidewall and the frame or leaf springs on the inside, and an inch between the tire and fender lip on the outside. With the tires blocked to sit exactly where you want them, measure carefully from the backside of one wheel to the backside of the other. This is the axle-flange to axle-flange distance.

The second way of measuring starts with the fender lip-to-fender lip distance, minus clearance between tire and fender times two, minus the front offset of each wheel times two. If it all sounds confusing, it is. Talk to the person or shop that is narrowing your rear end and measure it the way they want you to—with a sketch so everyone understands the measurements. That way there won't be any miscommunication.

Axles can't be cut and welded, they must be cut to the correct length and then resplined. If you are working with the larger diameter axles in 28 splines they can be resplined to 31 splines for more strength. This means, of course, that the 28-spline side gears will no longer work. In some cases it also means a little machine work as the hole in the ring gear carrier may be too small for the larger 31-spline axle.

The rear-end housing itself is cut approximately 2in from the outer flange, so the area where the wheel bearing mounts is left intact. Then the correct amount of housing is cut off on each side to create the new, narrowed rear-end housing. Usually, any offset from side to side is left intact, and equal amounts are removed from each side of the housing. (If you have any doubt about how much should be taken off each side, check the driveshaft tunnel in the car and make sure the new, narrowed rear end will

put the driveshaft in the center of the tunnel.) Before welding the end flanges back on, however, there's another step.

Welding the suspension brackets onto the housing will probably cause the housing to warp. Warped housings are very hard on wheel bearings and tires (and also quite common), so you should stop now, before having the end flanges welded onto the housing.

The idea is to temporarily bolt the axle housing and third-member into the car, correctly figure the U-joint angles, and then weld on the necessary suspension brackets or spring pads. After welding the brackets onto the housing, the axle housing itself should go back to the shop with the alignment fixture. Final welding of the axle housing ends should be done with the alignment fixture in place. That way you know the axles and tires run absolutely true. When the brackets or pads are welded on *after* welding up the housing, the housing is often warped as a result.

So, if you can't find one of the rare Granada-Lincoln rear ends, then buy the biggest one you can find. Plan to spend plenty of time (or money) looking for a good used positraction unit. And follow all the steps outlined above when narrowing a rear end and welding on new saddle brackets.

And the Alternatives Are:

If a 9in is too hard to find or too expensive, there are of course a host of other choices. A short and incomplete list would start with the 8in Ford rear end used in many mid-size Ford products. Though not as durable as the 9in, this is a perfectly good rear end and it is a third-member design. Some of these Ford rear ends are only 56in wide, flange to flange, which means they fit many Deuces and later street rods without narrowing. Some of these came with factory disc brakes, another nice feature.

In the GM line, the smaller 10-bolt rear end used in many Novas and similar products is popular,

continued on next page

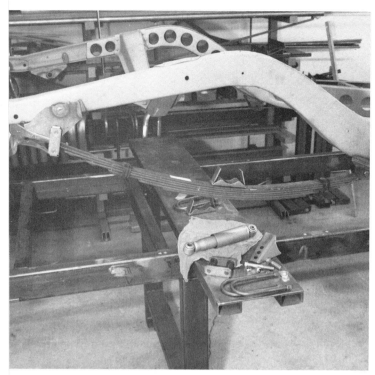

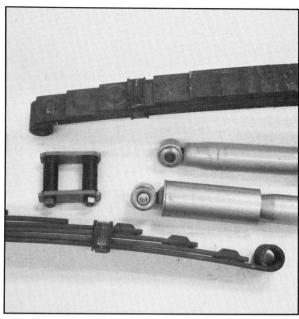

Springs hanging in the no-load position. Simple axle mounting saddle is supplied with the spring kit.

These are the Posies springs with Super Slide buttons, shackles, and shocks. The springs don't have much arch and are designed to keep the car low without the use of lowering blocks. When buying a rear spring kit, be sure to ask how low it will put your car and the exact location of the rear wheels in the wheelwell or fender.

There's more than one way to get the suspension to ride height. Here the springs are compressed before the pinion angle is determined and the axle saddles are welded in place.

With the suspension loaded, Jim checks each side against the frame centerline and against the dimensions that were determined during the planning process—before welding on the axle saddles.

Just one more step before welding on those saddles—Jim sets the pinion angle.

The saddles have been welded in place. Use some caution when welding on the saddles to avoid too much heat and a warped axle housing.

and the height positions are known, the wheel flange is bolted to a fixture so the remaining linkage can be mounted in place. When he mounts the hub to the fixture, Larry always checks the camber of the hub to be sure it is mounted straight in the fixture.

Putting the two parallel rods in place is pretty straightforward once the hub is bolted in at the ride height. These two rods should be parallel to one another and roughly parallel to the ground.

Mounting a Plain, Old Straight Axle and Leaf Springs

The first step in a situation like this is the mounting of the new leaf springs. A large variety of companies offer quality kits to convert Henry's buggy-style cross-spring rear suspension to a pair of leaf springs. If you're building a rod from a Chevrolet product, and those old narrow rear leaf springs just aren't up to the task, new ones are available from a variety of suppliers. Open a catalog and order a new kit, with improved springs and all the hardware needed to install new leaf springs under your Chevy (and most other brands as well). Many of these springs are already de-arched to keep the height nice and low, while offering a much stronger spring than those old originals.

The finished installation—upper shock mounts weld directly to the cross-member while the lower brackets are welded to the lower U-bolt plates.

Mounting a new set of springs starts (again) with the setup of the frame on a table of some kind. Get the frame at ride height and find the axle centerline (fat Fords use an axle snubber that marks the centerline of the axle). After removing the old spring mounts where necessary, simply mount the spring perches per the locations that come with the new spring kits. Use a carpenter's square to ensure that the new perches end up with the mounting holes for the springs parallel to the ground (don't assume the sides of the rails are 90deg to the ground). You probably want to box the frame rails where the perches mount or at least weld in a reinforcing tab to help support the weight where the spring perch mounts on the frame.

In order to simulate ride height or a load on the car, some builders put the springs in with only the main leaf, just to see how everything really lines up, how much clearance there is between the axle and the frame, and where the tire will be positioned in the wheelwell. You will have to run the suspension through full compression and rebound to correctly figure the shock mounting. In general, the shocks should mount with two-thirds of their movement in compression and one-third in rebound (starting from

To illustrate a four-bar rear suspension installation we chose a kit from Pete and Jake's—although there are numerous manufacturers that make similar kits. The kit includes the bars, and brackets for both ends. A panhard rod (not shown) should be used with parallel four-bar suspension systems.

The instructions gave an exact location for the front brackets so Jim tack welded these to the frame rails. Some kits suggest you correctly position the rear end up under the frame with the four-bar brackets attached and then work forward.

A plumb bob is a very handy thing to have in the shop. It is used here to check the axle location against the intended centerline marked on the table. This frame is unfinished and was pressed into service to illustrate the four-bar installation.

Like the brackets used on a front four-bar suspension, these have to be positioned perfectly. Small errors in the location of one or both brackets will make large errors in the way everything else is positioned. Here Jim checks the bracket location against the wheelbase. The bracket height and distance from the frame centerline must be checked too.

Measure twice, weld once. Jim double-checks the location of the brackets and the alignment of the four-bars.

ride height). Most manufacturers suggest that shocks be mounted at up to 30deg from vertical at ride height. Be sure to add axle snubbers that stop the axle movement on compression at least ½in before the shock absorbers bottom out.

Mounting a Four-Bar Rear Suspension

The kit illustrated here is from Pete and Jake's, installed in a Model A frame at the Metal Fab shop. You're probably tired of being told to "set up the frame on a level table and work at ride height," so we'll delete that part.

Like the installation of a four-bar system on the front, there are two basic approaches when putting four-bars on the rear. If the kit gives dimensions for the location of the four-bar brackets, you can tack weld them on the frame, install the axle housing and the bars and then see where everything ends up relative to the axle centerline already marked on the frame and table. Or, you can set the axle up under the frame, using a fixture of some kind to hold it correctly, and then just weld in the brackets wherever they end up on the frame rails (in the front-to-rear dimension).

In this case we chose to tack weld the brackets onto the frame first per the instruction sheet. Next, the rear end was mounted up under the frame using the axle centerline, ride height, and frame centerline as the references.

The frame brackets (no matter which method you use to locate them) need to be positioned so the

bolt holes are level with the ground. Be sure the brackets are both the same distance from the ground, the same distance from the frame centerline, and the same distance from the axle centerline. These brackets need to be installed correctly—and they also need to be in exactly the same

It's easy to install the rear end off to one side just a little bit—and create a surprisingly large weight imbalance. So check the rear end position carefully against the frame centerline.

position on both sides. Small errors in the location of the mounting brackets are magnified and will require a lot of adjustment to correct later.

The pinion angle should be adjusted before the axle brackets are welded to the rear axle. Use a protractor and set the angle per the illustrations and notes in the engine installation chapter. By setting the pinion angle before welding on the axle brackets, we again save the threaded adjusters for use later.

After setting the pinion angle, tack weld on the axle brackets, install the four-bars and see how everything stacks up. Check the rear axle position against the front axle centerline and the frame centerline, then double-check the pinion angle (remember Jim's comment of working in three dimensions). The four-bars should end up adjusted so most of the threads are screwed into the rod and only a few threads are showing. Ideally, each bar has roughly the same number of threads showing.

By moving the axle up and down through full suspension movement, you can check for any binding in the linkage and determine the dimensions for the shock absorbers. You need two-thirds of the movement on compression and one-third on rebound. Don't let the shock act as the axle stop on compression or those expensive coil-overs won't last very long. Always install the upper shock brackets after the axle has been adjusted for pinion angle, and keep the upper and lower mounts parallel.

The only thing left is the panhard rod, and the installation will vary slightly depending on the car and the individual kit.

Final welding can be done after all the dimensions have been checked one more time. When the brackets are welded onto the rear axle, it's a good idea to have it done with a heli-arc as this creates less heat and less chance of warping the rear-end housing.

With everything at ride height, you can measure the distance needed for the shock absorber. The compressed and extended distances should be checked as well.

The multiple holes in the lower bracket make it easier to find a pair of shocks that fit correctly. Most shops install shocks at about (but not more than) a thirty degree lean at ride height.

Chapter 5

Brakes

Theory

Considering Brake Designs

First, a short discussion of brakes and what they really do.

In reality, your brakes are just heat machines. In high school physics they taught us the first law of thermodynamics. In case high school was more than just a few years ago, the law goes like this: *You cannot create or destroy energy, you can only convert it from one form to another.* A moving car has considerable kinetic energy. When you apply the brakes you turn that kinetic, or moving, energy into heat energy.

The formula for kinetic energy (another leftover from those early science classes) states that kinetic energy equals weight times speed squared, divided by 29.9. Don't get turned off by the formula, the idea is to make you understand just a couple of things about kinetic energy. First, when you double the weight you double the kinetic energy. Second and more important, when you double the speed you create four times the kinetic energy.

As you add weight and speed, you need more brakes. More, in this case, means more rotor and more caliper to deal with all the energy (read: heat).

Larger rotors are better and work to your advantage in three ways: by providing a larger total surface area, by providing more leverage for the caliper to work on, and by providing more total mass to handle more total heat. A ventilated rotor usually has more mass to handle the heat, and the ventilation running through the center of the rotor helps keep it cool. A larger caliper (within reason) provides a larger piston and pad to better grab that big rotor, and more mass to deal with and absorb the heat.

So far the discussion has included only disc brakes. That's because disc brakes are much better than drum brakes in most situations. Yes, nostalgia Deuce coupes look good with finned Buick brake drums on the front and those big Buick brakes do a fine job of slowing down a little coupe. Yet, when there's a choice between drum and disc, and there are no overriding visual factors, the choice should be disc brakes. Especially on the front of your car.

As street rods get heavier there is an increased need for better brakes. Posies offers this conversion kit for cars running Mustang II spindles. The kit includes 11in Grenada rotors (5x4 1/2in bolt pattern) mated to mid-size GM single-piston calipers. Posies

For street rods with a 1937-41 Ford spindle, Posies offers this kit with vented rotors (to better handle the heat) and GM calipers. Posies

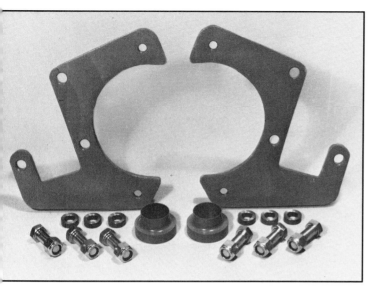

The folks at ECI feel that the proportioning valve, like this one, is the one component left out of most street rod brake conversions. ECI

More disc brake conversion kits come on the market every year. These brackets from Engineered Components Inc. (ECI) will put disc brakes on 1937-48 Ford cars and 1937-56 pickup trucks. ECI

Offered by ECI, this Corvette dual-disc master cylinder is mated to a new power booster of only 7in diameter to better fit under the floor of your street rod. If you want power brakes, do it this way, with an integral power unit mounted at the master cylinder. ECI

Why are disc brakes so much better than drum brakes? There are at least three good reasons: First, disc brakes put the friction surface right out there where the air can get at it and help to keep it cool. Second, any dirt or water that hits the spinning rotor tends to be thrown off, a nice self-cleaning feature. Third, disc brakes offer a greater surface area for a given amount of weight as compared to drum brakes.

The brakes on your car are part of a hydraulic system and it's hard to talk about the brakes without backing up to talk about hydraulics and basic hydraulic laws. A master cylinder with a small piston will create a lot of pressure (pressure = force divided by area). That's great you say, I'll run a small-diameter piston in the master cylinder to create a lot of pressure and won't need a power booster. There is, however, a trade-off in using a small diameter piston. A small piston doesn't move as much fluid and the pedal may be right on the floor when you've actually moved the pedal far enough to displace enough fluid to push the pads against the rotor.

Without further discussion of physics and formulas which no one wants to read anyway, consider that there must be a good match between the master cylinder and the calipers or wheel cylinders. You can't just go to smaller and smaller diameter master cylinder pistons or bigger and bigger caliper pistons. (The fluid pressure created by the master cylinder works on the area of the caliper or wheel cylinder pistons. So the bigger the area of the caliper piston the more force created by a given pressure.)

In the real world you probably want more pressure but still need to displace a certain volume of fluid. A power booster may be the perfect compromise—more hydraulic pressure without any loss in the amount of fluid displaced. Remember, too, that the area of a piston is pi (3.14159) times the radius squared, so very small changes in the radius result in large changes in the area.

Before leaving this discussion of brake design, it might be instructive to consider the ideal balance between front and rear brakes (whether it's four-wheel discs or not) and how that balance is achieved.

We all know that Detroit uses a proportioning valve between the front and rear brakes to help balance out a disc/drum brake system. That proportioning valve does more than "balance" the brakes, in fact in most cases it has two jobs.

The basic problem with using disc brakes on the fronts and drums in the rear is two-fold. First, the drum brakes, with their big shoes, big return springs, and relatively large distance between the shoes and the drum, require something like 125psi to actually force the shoes against the drums with enough force

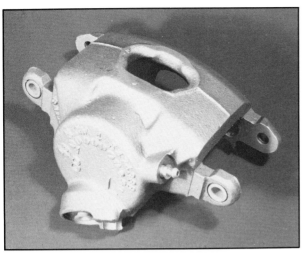

These rebuilt mid-size GM calipers are available from ECI (and others) and have become very popular with street rodders converting their rods to disc brakes on the front axle. Beware of used calipers that have been sitting for years. ECI

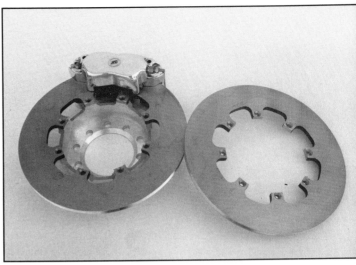

Aftermarket brakes like these from JFZ often use "hats" to adapt a particular rotor to a particular hub. Non-vented rotors like these are only safe on light cars or the rear axle. JFZ

This deluxe kit from ECI uses Corvette aluminum calipers (from the 1984 and later Corvettes) and a vented rotor to do a great job of stopping street rods of up to 4,500lbs. ECI

109

To solve the problem of how to get an emergency brake when you have aftermarket rear discs, Wilwood offers a small, mechanical caliper that can be mounted in conjunction with their other hydraulic calipers. Heidt's

to slow down the car. Disc brakes, on the other hand, need only about one-tenth as much pressure to push the pads against the rotor with enough force to affect the car's speed.

So the first job of the factory proportioning valve is to "hold off" the front brakes until the system reaches approximately 125psi. In this way the car uses both the front and rear brakes to do the stopping, even in light applications.

The second job of the proportioning valve is to actually proportion the pressure to the rear brakes, depending on how hard you stop. Understanding

this second function requires us to look at how the car reacts in two very different stopping situations. In an easy stop from slow speed, there is little weight transfer and the rear tires maintain good traction during the stop. In this stop, the pressure in the system rises to a modest level until the brakes apply and the car stops. During this stop the hydraulic pressure to the front and rear is the same.

Now, imagine the same car stopping hard from high speed. In this case there is a great deal of weight transfer onto the front tires. This leaves the rear tires with little traction and in danger of locking

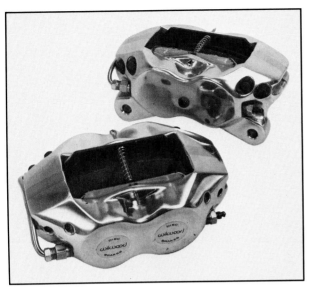

Available from Heidt's, these polished four-piston calipers from Wilwood look great on street rods. Heidt's

up. In this situation the proportioning valve limits the hydraulic pressure that is applied to the rear brakes in order to prevent the rear tires from locking up.

Now that you know everything there is to know about brake design, it's time to consider the right system for your car.

Theory

Buying a System for Your Car

Before running out to the parts store or rod shop to buy the brake parts for your new ride, it might be instructive to consider first what you want and second, what you actually need. Third, of course, is what you can *afford.*

The importance of the brakes can't be over-stated and few street rod builders would consciously skimp on their brakes. The problem is not so much a matter of bad equipment. Most of the equipment out there, whether it's from Detroit or the after-market, is of very high quality. Rather, the problem comes from equipment that is poorly matched to the job at hand.

In case it needs to be stated, the job at hand is stopping and slowing the car during street driving (remember, these are *street* rods). They may be hot rods but they are not race cars. Though the race car stuff may look impressive, it doesn't always work better than—or even as well as—components and systems designed for street use and that includes good, old OEM stuff from Detroit.

What you buy will depend on your budget, bolt pattern, spindle, style of car, and its weight. In general, you want to buy as much brake as you can for a given amount of cash. An engineer once explained to me: "When you're considering brakes,

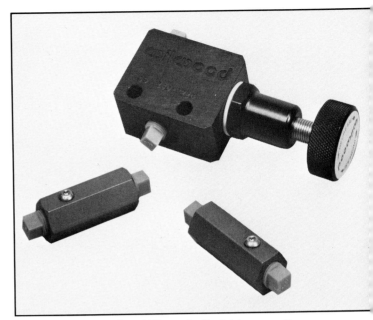

Offered by Heidt's, these Wilwood adjustable proportioning valves and residual check valves (in 2 and 10lb ratings) are used on many street rods. Heidt's

more is usually better. More surface area, more pistons, and larger calipers."

We have already stated a strong bias in favor of disc brakes. As the front brakes do seventy percent (or more) of the stopping in a hard stop, it makes sense to put your best foot forward. Like Detroit, you may want to run discs in the front and drums at the rear.

Buying brakes can be broken down roughly into OEM-style and aftermarket. Ralph Lisena, owner of Engineered Components Incorporated (ECI) had some interesting comments regarding the choice of components for a street rod brake system. Since Ralph has been at this game of street rod brakes for thirteen years now, his comments bear repeating:

"People don't want to admit it, but the engineers from Detroit do a pretty good job. When they design a system for a car, that system works and it exhibits good balance. If people would just use a Detroit system, one that's big enough for the weight of their car, and not mix it with a lot of aftermarket components, they wouldn't get in so much trouble. If they do want to use a JFZ or Wilwood or someone else's components, then they should buy as much of that system as they can from that company. Before the purchase they should be sure to talk to a sales representative from the *manufacturer* to be sure that the components they intend to use are all intended to work together and that they are all intended for street applications.

"People get in trouble with their street rod brakes because they mis-match a variety of components from different manufacturers—some of it OEM and some of it from the aftermarket. They also

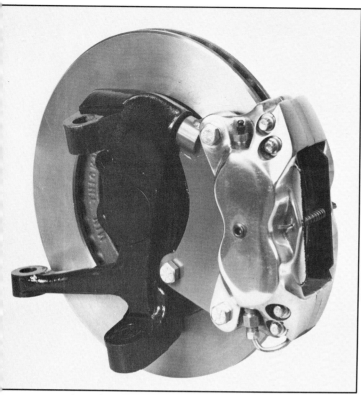

These brackets from Heidt's mate a variety of calipers to the Mustang II and Superide front spindles. Heidt's

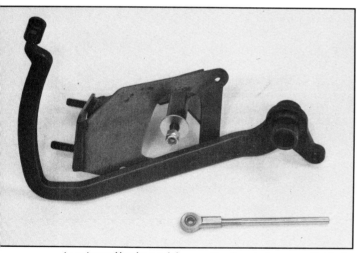

A variety of brake pedal mounting brackets are available for nearly any street rod.

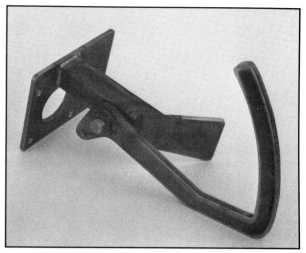

Another brake pedal assembly, one which is often used in Boyd's shop. This is a very sturdy bracket, especially if it's tied into the X-member.

get in trouble because they use little 9in rotors on the front of their car. Their '40 Ford with a Mustang clip or Mustang style independent front suspension might weigh 3,200lbs. That doesn't seem like much weight so they figure the small, 9in rotors and Ford calipers will work just fine. And they do—until you put two people and their gear in the car and maybe hang a little trailer on the back. Now you're up near 4,000lbs, and there aren't *any* 4,000lb Mustangs."

Ralph went on to explain: "Street rodders who aren't going to spend the money for some real sexy brake system should pick a system from a Detroit car that weighs the same or a little more than their street rod, and then use the whole system. The front brakes, the rear brakes, the master cylinder, and the proportioning valve."

By using the correct master cylinder with a Detroit brake system, you avoid problems with mismatching the master cylinder to the style of brakes that are used. Drum brakes need a 10lb to 12lb residual-pressure check valve in the hydraulic system (usually built into the master cylinder). This pressure keeps the lips of the cups expanded out against the wheel cylinder bore and prevents air ingestion past the wheel cylinder cups when you release the brake pedal.

That same 10lb residual check valve used on a disc brake system will cause the brakes to drag. The only time you need a check valve on a disc brake system is when the master cylinder is mounted lower than the calipers—the valve (a 2lb check valve in this case) prevents all the fluid in the caliper from siphoning back to the master cylinder.

The proportioning valve that came from the donor car will probably work on your street rod, except in cases where the rear of the street rod is very light—like a Bucket T or Model A pickup truck—and the proportioning valve is designed for a car with a higher percentage of the weight on the rear axle. In these cases you may need one of the adjustable proportioning valves. If the donor car is relatively old (as is usually the case or it wouldn't be "donating" anything) you probably want to buy a new proportioning valve, without all the rust and crud that's trapped in the old one.

So whatever components you use, try to make them all part of a system that is designed to work

This is the neat master cylinder mounting on Gene Younk's Buick. Note the integral power booster, adjustable proportioning valve, and well-supported booster mounting bracket. Note too the dual-chamber master cylinder—don't use the old fruit jar anymore.

together. If you decide to use the later model Corvette brakes (1984 and later), use a Corvette master cylinder meant to work with those calipers. Speaking of master cylinders, there is no excuse for using a single master cylinder on a street rod—not anymore. Always use a split master, that way if you blow a hose or run half the system out of fluid you still have some brakes.

The brake lines you use will depend partly on the components that make up your brake system. Some of the newer cars from Detroit use ¼in lines to the front calipers because the calipers require a relatively large volume of fluid to move the pistons. In other situations the old standard, ³⁄₁₆in lines, are probably more than adequate.

If the components you intend to install are used, be sure to have the hydraulic components overhauled. Calipers should be overhauled with new inner seals and outer dust boots. Single piston calipers use a floating mechanism so that the force of one piston is transmitted evenly to two brake pads. If the pins or sliding surface aren't clean, then they don't "float" and prematurely wear only one of the brake pads. Calipers that don't float will drag and overheat or warp the rotors.

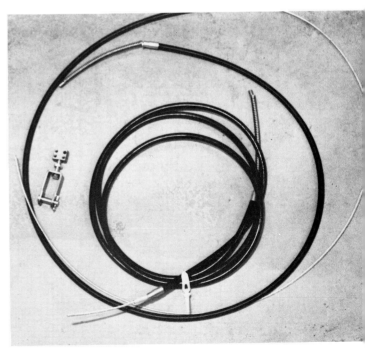

Always use new E-brake cables and hardware when installing emergency brakes in your car.

The rest of the brakes for Gene's Buick. Front calipers are aftermarket, mated to Ford rear calipers.

Here Gene's polished calipers are bolted onto the car, ready to squeeze the 11in vented rotors.

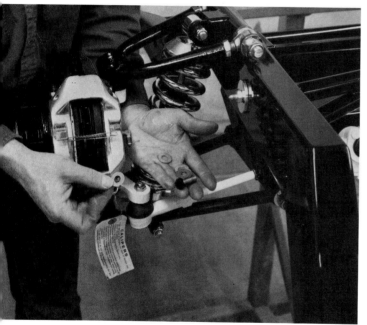

When aftermarket calipers are used they often must be shimmed at the mount to get the caliper centered over the rotor. Jim Petrykowski has the shims and mounting bolts in his hand.

When all the components are installed and you're ready to bleed the system, you might figure the tough decisions are over—until you get to the auto parts store and see at least three grades of brake fluid on the shelf. What to do? Well, first, let's consider what the brake fluid actually does.

Brake fluid is nothing more than specialized hydraulic fluid operating in a very specialized hydraulic system. The brake system must follow basic hydraulic laws: (1) A fluid cannot be compressed to a smaller volume; and (2) pressure in the system is equal over all surfaces of the system (assume for the moment that there is no proportioning valve).

What this means is that the pressure at the master cylinder outlet during a stop is applied fully to the pistons in the calipers and not in compressing the fluid link between the master cylinder and the calipers. It also means that the pressure at the master cylinder outlet is the same pressure that is applied to all the surfaces (read pistons) in the brake system.

Brake fluid is simply a very specialized hydraulic fluid. One that operates in a very dirty environment and must withstand very high temperatures without boiling. When brake fluid boils, the fluid becomes a gas (a compressible material). The driver senses this as a spongy brake pedal. So brake fluid must stay viscous at nearly any temperature and resist boiling up to at least 400 degrees Fahrenheit.

There are three grades of brake fluid commonly available and graded by the US Department of Transportation (DOT): DOT 3, DOT 4 and DOT 5. DOT 3 and 4 are glycol-based fluids with dry boiling points of 401 and 446 degrees Fahrenheit, respectively. Either fluid is suitable for use in disc brake systems. There are two basic problems with DOT 3 and DOT 4 brake fluids: they tend to absorb water from the environment (they are hydroscopic) and they make a great paint remover.

If you are using glycol-based brake fluid, remember to keep the container closed so it won't pick up moisture from the air, and be careful to avoid spilling any on that new paint job. Because the DOT 3 or 4 brake fluid in your car will pick up some water no matter how careful you are, it's a good idea to flush the system with fresh fluid every couple of years. Remember that brake fluid contaminated with water boils at a much lower temperature and can be corrosive to pistons and cylinder bores.

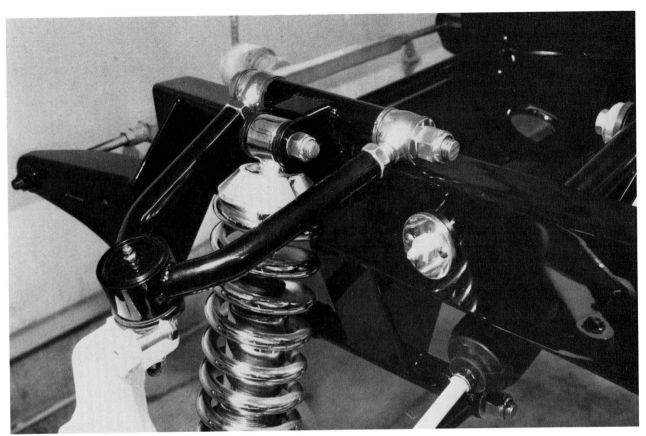

Gene likes things very neat. The brake lines are mounted inside the frame, exiting through the polished bracket.

Some of the problems inherent in DOT 3 and 4 brake fluids are overcome by DOT 5 brake fluid. DOT 5 fluid is silicone based, meaning a higher boiling point (500 degrees Fahrenheit, dry), no tendency to absorb water, and no reaction when spilled on a painted surface (though silicone fluid can stain the paint if not washed off quickly).

Like every other advance, silicone brake fluid has its trade-offs. In fact, silicone isn't everyone's favorite brake fluid. Silicone costs more, it is slightly compressible, it aerates more easily than glycol-based fluid, and it is said to cause swelling of the cups and seals used in brake systems after long-term exposure. The choice is yours, but no matter which fluid you decide to use, stick with it and do not mix one brake fluid type with another.

When you plan your brake system, you also need to plan for an emergency brake. Though there are a number of retro-fit types of hydraulic emergency brake systems out there, the best system may well be one used by Detroit. If you're using stock drum brakes in the rear, then all you have to do is hook up the cables. If you want four-wheel disc brakes, then the choice of rear calipers will affect your options for an emergency brake.

Rear disc brake calipers fall into two categories: those with and those without an integral emergency

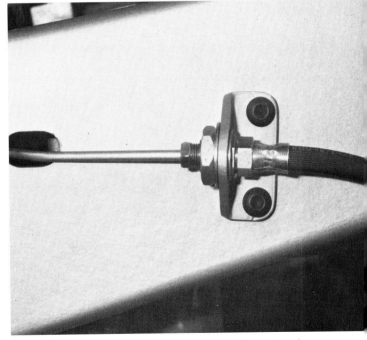

Jim Prokop's Dodge. Note the bracket and the relatively large hole where the brake line runs through the frame. Be sure all your brake lines are well clamped so they don't vibrate and crack.

This simple brake pedal bracket was fabricated in the Metal Fab shop. A simple design, well supported, and easy to make.

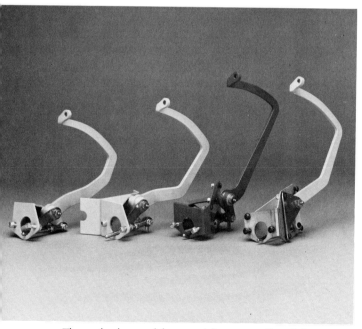

These brake pedal assemblies are offered by TCI in different styles to fit most street rods. TCI

brake. Most of the calipers with an integral emergency brake are from Detroit and there are only a few to choose from.

One popular candidate for Detroit-supplied disc brake calipers is from the Corvette. Corvettes have used four-wheel disc brakes for years, although all Corvette systems are not created equal. The calipers used on pre-1984 Corvettes have a host of problems all their own, and should probably be avoided altogether. In 1984 the Corvette got a major redesign, and that redesign included new brakes. These four-wheel discs are some of the best in the world. The new single-piston calipers include a saddle assembly to reinforce the caliper body. Street rodders have been known to remove this saddle bracket to make the calipers fit certain wheels (especially 14in wheels). Removal of the saddle allows the calipers to flex and is a big no-no.

Back to the topic of emergency brakes, the 1984-87 Corvette rear calipers use a separate emergency brake made up of small shoes that expand against the inside of the rotor. A better choice for the street rodder looking for four-wheel disc brakes and easy emergency brakes is the 1988 and later Corvette

Aeroquip fittings and lines are very strong, but the flares are all thirty-seven degrees and thus can't be flared with a regular flare tool. Braided stainless lines are probably stronger than OEM yet they are not DOT approved and could be a red flag at a state inspection.

rear calipers since these feature a cable-operated emergency brake built into the caliper.

Other cars that use four-wheel discs and have the emergency brake as part of the rear caliper include some Camaros, Toronados, and Eldorados. In the Ford line, certain Lincoln Versailles and even some Granadas used the bulletproof 9in rear end with factory rear disc brakes and these calipers include integral emergency brakes.

If you decide to use aftermarket calipers on the rear axle, then you have to come up with your own emergency brake. Some people choose the additional rotor mounted at the rear U-joint, operated by its own caliper and master cylinder. Jim Petrykowski at Metal Fab warns that installing these systems correctly, without a lot of rotor runout, isn't always easy. You have to be sure that the caliper mounts solidly to the housing and that the rotor doesn't have much runout.

Another method is to mount an additional caliper on one or both of the rear rotors, operated by its own master cylinder. Small mechanical calipers are also available—meant for go-carts and such—and could be mounted in tandem with the existing calipers on the rear brakes.

This may be another situation where planning pays big dividends. By planning ahead and choosing a combination of rear brake rotor and caliper with integral E-brake, a lot of headaches and time spent mounting a separate system can be avoided.

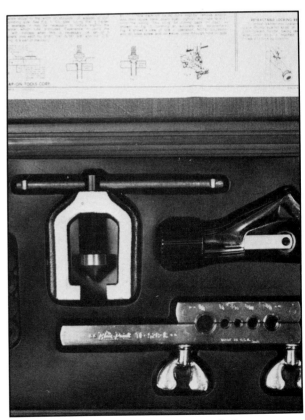

This double-flare tool from Snap-On will do most standard double-flares on non-stainless steel tubing.

117

This odd-looking tool is a rotary burnishing tool and it will do a nice thirty-seven degree flare as used with the Aeroquip system. No, it's not cheap.

The Ford frame seen in suspension chapters 3 and 4, with its power booster and Corvette master cylinder. This cylinder can be converted to use with rear drum brakes with the addition of the right Detroit-style proportioning valve.

Those polished calipers and trick hubs sure look neat on the front of a street rod—but remember to buy hubs that use standard easy-to-find bearings for that occasional breakdown in Podunk, Iowa, on Sunday afternoon.

Corvette calipers on a street rod frame. These calipers work very well and may not be as expensive as you think.

Hands-On

Installing the Brakes

First, a short warning: When working on your brakes you must adhere to all the procedures followed by any good mechanic. This includes careful assembly, attention to detail, extreme cleanliness when dealing with the hydraulic part of the system, careful examination after the work is finished to check for leaks, and a careful road test. Remember that solvents attack the rubber used as seals in brake systems so all cleaning of hydraulic parts must be done with clean brake fluid.

There is nothing worse for a brake system or component than sitting. When you drag that old rear end out of the junk yard—where it's been sitting for years—force the wheel cylinders apart and overhaul or replace each one. Master cylinders also should be overhauled or simply replaced with new components. Calipers must be forced apart (use compressed air to force the piston from the bore), the parts cleaned and inspected. Pitted pistons need to be replaced, and the caliper bore should be thoroughly cleaned and sanded with some light sandpaper or a brake hone if you have one that's big enough.

Rebuilt calipers are available from a variety of sources at pretty reasonable prices. If you decide to overhaul your own calipers, do a thorough job. Where people get in trouble is by not cleaning the groove for the square seal. Once that seal is removed, use a scribe or bend up a little tool from a welding rod, and clean, clean, clean that groove. When all the dirt and rust are removed, lubricate the new seal with clean brake fluid before popping it into the groove in the caliper. Lubricate the piston, too, before sliding it into the bore. Be sure to clean the groove for the dust boot so it seats correctly and does a good job of keeping everything clean and dry.

As already mentioned, most OEM calipers are single-piston designs that float. If the pins (on GM calipers) or the sliding surfaces are dirty and rusty, the caliper can't float. Be sure to clean all sliding surfaces, and replace the pins on GM calipers if they're rusty.

Front Brakes

If the front brakes are discs, you need to install the rotors, caliper brackets, and the calipers themselves. Used rotors should be turned on a lathe, and checked against the factory specifications to see that there is still enough material left on the rotor after

A dual-chamber master cylinder is the only way to go. You might say that it will "never happen to you" but it can. The bracket is tied into the X-member for good support.

turning. Be sure to clean all the old grease (and metal filings from the lathe) out of the hub, inspect the bearing races, pack the bearings, and use a new seal when you put everything together.

Caliper brackets should be original or come from a good aftermarket supplier. Remember that the full force of a panic stop is transmitted to the chassis through that caliper bracket. So don't skimp, use a good bracket and bolt it to the spindle assembly with grade eight bolts.

Many of the popular front brake kits for the Mustang II and even some early Ford axles combine a mid-size GM caliper with an 11in ventilated rotor. In most cases the rotor is thinner than the stock GM rotor (most of these rotors are 0.810in thick while the original was 0.960in), and that's why some of these kits also supply a spacer to be used behind the inner brake pad. If you leave out the spacer, the piston comes out farther than the GM engineers intended. This might be all right until the pads become worn— when the end of the piston is pushed past the inner seal and you lose the front brakes.

If you are mounting an aftermarket caliper, it probably came with a series of small spacers. You will have to experiment with these until the caliper is centered over the disc rotor.

Mount your new or rebuilt caliper to the caliper bracket and get ready to hook up the hoses. Hoses that came from the donor car should probably be discarded and replaced with new hoses. Be careful in your choice of hoses and brackets. It's easy to install a hose that's too short or too long—a hose that will tear on a bump or rub on a tire. After installing the new hoses, run the suspension up and down, and back and forth to check for any clearance problems.

When mounting calipers on your car, be sure that the bleeder screw ends up at the top of the caliper. If not, you will have to bleed the brakes with the calipers held so the bleeder is on top, with a large socket or something stuck between the pads to take the place of the rotor.

Braided lines look great and may be stronger than stock flexible lines. Most, however, are not DOT approved and may cause your car to fail a state inspection (something to think about).

As this sport or hobby of ours evolves, the cars get more and more sophisticated. Some of the professional and advanced amateur builders are running the brake lines inside the frame rails. That's really not necessary unless you're going to the "nth" degree with everything else. What *is* important is the little brackets and clamps you use to clamp the brake lines to the frame rails. Loose brake lines vibrate, crack, and rub on the chassis. The only good brake line is one that's clamped in place by any of the various means available to the modern street rodder. Be sure to use grommets where the line passes through an opening in the frame or body and keep the lines away from any heat source.

It may not need to be said (I'll say it anyway) but only genuine brake lines and materials intended for brake lines should be used. A panic stop can generate as much as 1,000psi in the hydraulic system—too much pressure for anything but an approved steel brake line, with double-flare fittings or systems specifically designed for automotive brakes.

Stainless steel lines *are* available, although it may be a case of overkill. A stainless line may last forever, but they are very hard to bend and harder still to double flare.

Rear Brakes

If you're using disc brakes at the rear, then the installation follows the outline just presented. Be sure the caliper brackets are heavy enough. Use new flexible lines anytime there's a doubt and make sure the lines don't rub on anything.

Drum brakes need a little TLC for correct operation. Be sure to turn any used drums and make sure they aren't beyond the specification from being turned too many times. Shoes should be new, and wheel cylinders need to be overhauled or replaced with new ones. The hardware and springs that hold and retract the shoes should probably be replaced at the same time you're doing all the other work.

Mounting the Master Cylinder and Brake Pedal Assembly

Most street rods mount the master cylinder to the frame, under the floor. This keeps everything mounted to the frame, and all that hardware off the firewall. A variety of mounting brackets are available, or the enterprising builder can fabricate his or her own.

The master cylinder bracket needs to be sturdy so the full movement of the pedal is transmitted to piston movement and not causing flexing of the mounting bracket. Many builders mount the bracket solidly to the left frame rail and then find a way (easier on some cars than others) to tie the bracket to the X-member or one of the cross-members. While the master cylinder and booster need to be below

floor level, you don't want them any lower than necessary.

If you use a vacuum-operated power booster, be sure to use a one-way valve in the vacuum line. Not only will this provide a more constant supply of vacuum to the diaphragm, it will keep gas vapors from seeping down the line (remember, they're heavier than air) and turning the brake booster into a potential bomb.

Be sure the centerline for the pedal pivot is perpendicular to the centerline of the car so the pedal moves straight and not through an arc. The master usually ends up mounted backwards from the way it was mounted in a Detroit car, so the hoses and reservoirs are backwards.

When the master cylinder that was meant to be mounted on the firewall with a swinging pedal is mounted under the floor, the pedal ratios often change. The overall mechanical advantage of the pedal may be about the same, but the pushrod now attaches at a point past the pivot for the brake pedal instead of between the pedal and its pivot. With the new underfloor arrangement, the pushrod often moves through more of an arc than it did in the old mounting position. This means that you have to be sure the pushrod pushes straight into the back of the master cylinder and doesn't hang up on the side of the master cylinder when the brakes are applied.

Ralph Lisena suggested that the pedal assembly and dry master cylinder be mounted on the bracket to be sure the pedal can move all the way to the floor without any hang-up in the linkage. This way, if you do lose half the hydraulic system, the pedal and pushrod *will* move far enough to engage the remaining hydraulic system.

Before you do the final mounting of the master cylinder, take a tip from professional mechanics: always "bench bleed" the master cylinder. Just use your fingers as one-way valves, allowing air and fluid to push past your fingertips when the pushrod is moved into the cylinder and sealing the outlets as the pushrod is allowed to come back to its rest position. When you mount the master in the car the job of bleeding the brakes will go about 101 percent faster because the master cylinder has already been bled.

A good brake system is well designed and carefully installed. It doesn't have to be sexy, it just has to do a good job of stopping the car. Fancy polished calipers with sixteen pistons won't stop the car unless they're well matched to the job at hand and the other components in the system. Think first, order second, and assemble with care.

Chapter 6

Shocks, Springs, and Coil-Overs

Introduction

Considering that a shock absorber is used at each corner of every street rod and considering further that coil-over shocks are used on a large percentage of street rods (at a cost of $200 per unit and up), it seems best to devote a complete chapter to the discussion of shocks and springs. We've all seen 'em, many of us have installed them, but how many of us really understand what a shock absorber does or how to correctly choose the right spring for the back of a Bucket T or a '34 Ford Sedan?

Theory

First, a look at shock absorbers and why you need them.

Take a spring that supports a weight. Compress the spring and let go. It doesn't just bounce back to its original position but rather goes through a series of oscillations, losing only a little movement with each up-and-down cycle.

If the spring in question is supporting your car, the up-and-down movement is unpleasant to the riders, to say the least (with certain exceptions). In order to dampen those oscillations, a shock absorber is attached at each corner of most cars. The first shock absorbers were just "friction" shocks rubbing a series of discs together to dampen out the up-and-down movement of early leaf springs. Hydraulic shocks were discovered early in the evolution of the automobile, but the relatively high cost kept

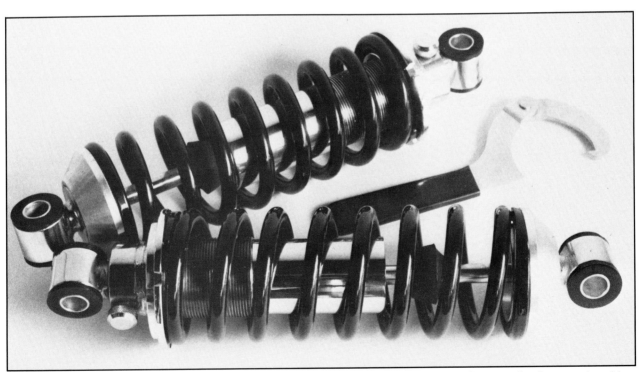

These Aldan coil-overs are rebuildable, something you might never do, yet it indicates a high-quality shock absorber. End bushings for most shocks come in rubber, urethane (better), and even heim-ends.

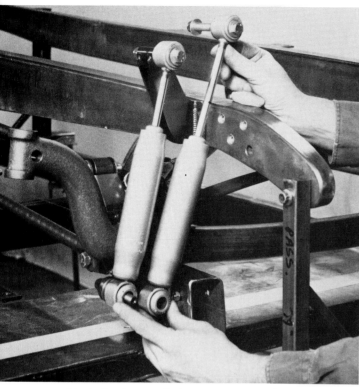

Most shock manufacturers recommend you mount the shocks so that at ride height there is still two-thirds of the travel left before the suspension bottoms. Here a fully extended shock is held next to one mounted at ride height.

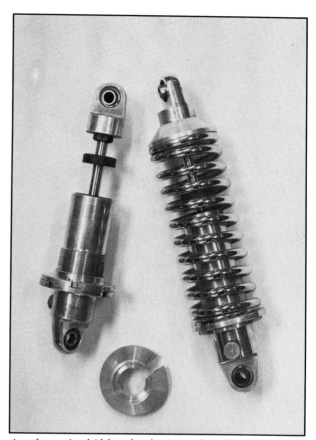

Another pair of Aldan shocks. Note the adjustment knob, the heim-ends, and the polished springs.

their use confined to the expensive brands. Henry Ford felt good shock absorbers were too important to ignore and insisted that the Deuce (an inexpensive car of the day) be equipped with Houdaille hydraulic shocks.

Anatomy of a Shock Absorber

Henry's early shocks were lever-action hydraulic shocks while most cars today are equipped with tubular shocks. Looking at a modern shock it's easy to imagine the piston attached to the pushrod, moving through a cylinder filled with oil.

Most shocks have a pair of valves located on the piston head. As the piston moves into the cylinder on compression, a valve is unseated to open an orifice or series of orifices and the oil passes through those little openings. When the shock goes into rebound, that first valve is closed and a different valve opens to allow the piston to move through the cylinder in the opposite direction, with the oil passing through a different set of openings.

The viscosity of the oil and the size of the holes that the oil passes through are the major factors affecting the stiffness of a particular shock absorber. By using different orifices for compression and rebound, a manufacturer is able to provide one level of stiffness on compression and another on re-

bound. For example, a typical Detroit sedan is equipped with shocks that are much softer on compression than they are on rebound—in order to achieve a good compromise between ride and suspension control. Street rod shock absorbers tend to be valved closer to fifty-fifty (the same on compression and rebound).

Most original equipment shock absorbers work just fine until the car hits a washboard gravel road at high speed. Soon the shock absorber pistons are moving through the fluid so fast and changing direction so often that a great deal of heat is created. The heat tends to change the viscosity of the oil, causing it to become thinner and reducing the effective stiffness of the shocks. Worse, as the piston changes direction rapidly it cavitates and soon there are air bubbles mixed with the oil. This aerated oil and air mixture isn't really oil at all. In this condition the shock is said to have "faded" and is contributing almost nothing to the control of the suspension.

Most of the problems encountered by a shock working overtime are overcome by the features found on most premium shock absorber designs. First, everything is a little larger and built to withstand additional loads. To better handle the heat, the amount of oil is increased. For better cooling, the body of the shock can be made of finned alumi-

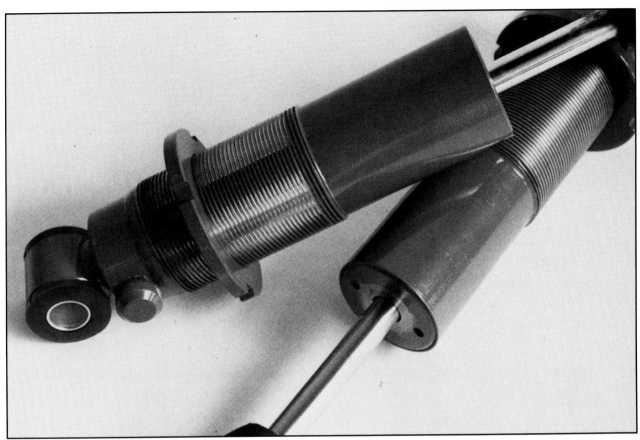

Buy quality shocks—make sure the threads are part of the shock body, not a collar welded onto the body. The screw-in cap on the top of the shock means it can be rebuilt, another indicator of quality.

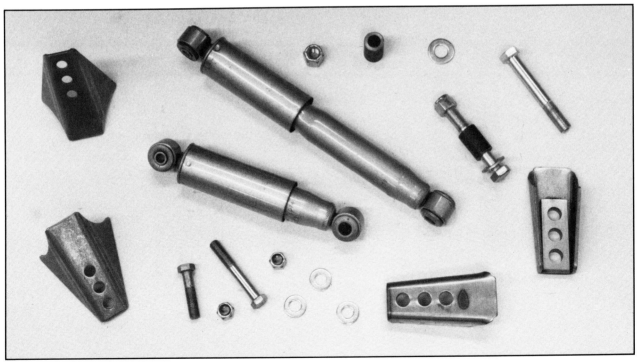

This is a simple and inexpensive shock kit available for the rear of many street rods with leaf springs.

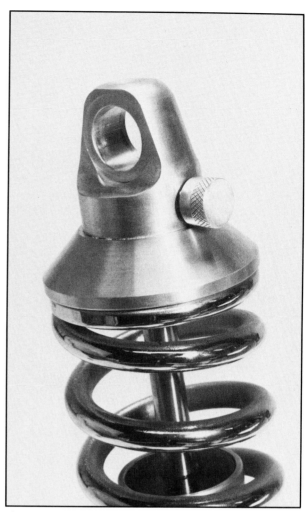

The new Eagle, a premium shock from Aldan. Features include an aluminum housing, adjustable valving (with the valve at the top for easier access), easy-turn spring adjustment collars, and of course it's gas-charged. Aldan

The adjustment knob on this Eagle shock allows you to fine-tune the compression damping to your personal tastes and the weight and design of your car. Aldan

num—to take advantage of aluminum's ability to quickly dissipate heat to the surrounding air. To reduce the tendency toward cavitation and the aeration of the oil, a pressure chamber is built into the shock and filled with nitrogen gas. By pressurizing the oil, the tendency toward aeration is reduced (much the way pressurizing the cooling system raises the boiling point of the antifreeze).

Yes, it might look like a simple tube filled with oil, but in reality a modern shock absorber is a very complex piece of equipment.

Anatomy of a Spring

Compared to a shock absorber, with its pistons and valves all working furiously on a bumpy road, a coil spring might seem the simplest thing in the world. Simple or not, there is more here than meets the proverbial eye.

Springs hold up the car, allowing suspension movement over bumps, and isolating (to varying

degrees) the occupants of the car from those lumps and bumps.

Coil springs are rated in pounds per inch—how many pounds of force it takes to compress the spring 1in. You could take the coil springs out of your Chevy coupe and test their ratings with a ruler and a bathroom scale. Most springs are linear in their strength. That is, if 200lbs will compress the spring 1in, then 400lbs will compress the same spring 2in (up to a certain limit, of course).

Determining the right spring for your car is mostly a matter of matching the spring rate with the weight of the car and the type of suspension.

Buying Shocks for Your Street Rod

As the president of one shock manufacturing company told me, "Street rodders have four things to consider when they choose a brand and model of shock: quality, convenience, performance, and aesthetics."

Mounted on a Model A frame, this coil-over is leaned over about how much? The angle of lean affects both the effective rate of the spring and the stiffness of the shock absorber.

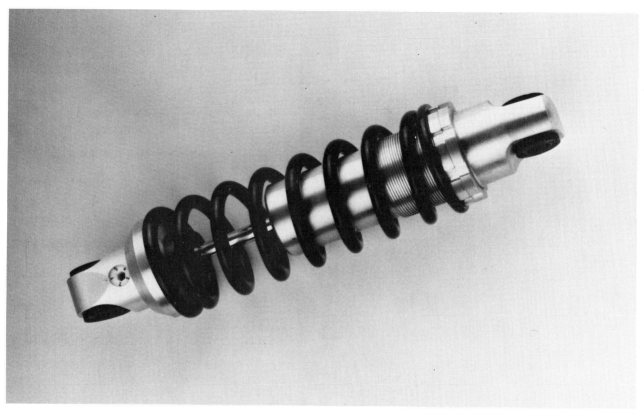

A relatively new contender in the coil-over market, this Viper shock is gas-charged and designed for street rods. The small hex opening on one end allows valving adjust- *ments and the body is cut from 6061 T6 aluminum. Pete and Jake's*

Most of the shock absorbers sold to the street rod industry, especially those designed to run as coil-overs, are already premium shock absorbers. When you go out to buy shocks, avoid Mickey Mouse coil-overs that aren't really coil-overs but rather just a standard car or truck shock absorber with a threaded collar tack welded to the shock body and a spring wrapped around it (more like an "overload" shock than a true coil-over). You want a shock that was designed as a coil-over. Buy a well-known brand name. Before choosing one from among the four or five really good brands out there, compare features and guarantees to decide which offers the best value.

Some shocks can be rebuilt. Although you may never need this feature, it does indicate a high-quality shock and also means the shock can be fine-tuned with different weight oil, for example, to suit your personal tastes.

Convenience includes the ease with which you can adjust the threaded collar and how easy it is to get at the adjustment for the valving (not all shocks are adjustable). Be sure there are plenty of springs available in different ratings to go along with the shock absorber.

Performance is related to quality. Find out if the shock is gas-charged. Gas-charged shocks usually

offer better performance and less chance that they will fade under tough duty. A gas-charged shock is usually of top quality. Note however, that because gas charged shocks are actually pressurized, they can raise the car by up to 1in.

Adjustable valving is a nice feature, as most companies only offer two basic shock absorber models for street rods (in various dimensions). The adjustable valving will allow you to fine-tune the shock's action to your personal taste and the weight of the vehicle. Most of the shocks only adjust on compression which is where most of us "feel" the difference in the shock absorber action (unless you spend considerably more for two-stage valving).

Aesthetics is perhaps the single most important issue with street rodders. Shocks are highly visible on many of our cars, and how the shock looks is a major part of the buying decision. An aluminum body makes for a nice-looking shock and the aluminum dissipates heat much better than steel. For most street rodders, the shock never actually gets hot enough to make the cooling properties of aluminum an important part of the decision.

Included in aesthetics is the overall finish of the shock mounting components and the look of the shock itself. Shocks built for street rodders usually have a large piston rod. Yes, it's a nice heavy-duty feature but most of the manufacturers do it just because, as the same shock manufacturer said, "Street rodders all seem to want a big rod."

Once you've chosen a price range, the important features, and a brand, getting the right shock with the right dimensions is a matter of knowing the dimensions at full compression, full extension, and ride height. Most manufacturers suggest that the shocks be installed so that one-third of the travel—from longest to shortest—is used at ride height. Stated another way, when mounted the shocks will be left with two-thirds of their movement in compression and one-third on rebound. (*Note:* One major manufacturer wants the shock mounted in the center of its travel at ride height.)

The shock absorber should never bottom out on compression. The suspension should be designed so that the axle or component hits the bump stop *before* the shock bottoms. Most manufacturers want the shock to have 1/2in of movement left when the suspension bottoms. The rubber collars seen on some shock absorber piston shafts are there as fail-safe features so that in a worst-case situation the piston head doesn't go blasting right down to the bottom of the bore.

Though the weight of your vehicle is important when choosing a shock, most manufacturers make the selection easy by offering shocks in two basic strengths—one for the front of the car and one for the rear. These two types come in a variety of lengths and mounting styles.

If you want something special, something other than the basic shock model offered by a particular manufacturer, then you can buy shocks with adjustable valving, or call the manufacturers to see if they have models (perhaps meant for the racetrack or special applications) that aren't in the street rod catalog.

The other option you have regarding the stiffness of the shock is in the way the shock is mounted. In general, the shocks should be mounted to be about 30deg from vertical at ride height. By mounting it more vertically, a shock becomes, in effect, stiffer; by mounting it in a more horizontal position, it becomes softer.

Buying Springs

Street rods (like most cars) use either leaf or coil springs. Buying leaf springs is pretty much a matter of matching your needs to the growing number of spring options in the catalogs.

In terms of strength and how high from the ground a particular spring will put your car, the best advice comes from the individual manufacturer. Many of the springs are available in standard form or de-arched to help get the car low and minimize the need for lowering blocks.

De-arching is an option for any leaf spring (and a better idea than removing individual leaves). You need to decide how much lower you want the car

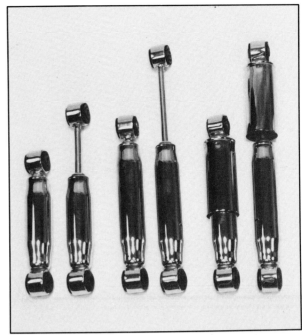

This selection of shock absorbers is offered by Posies to fit the front of nearly any street rod with a straight axle. Posies

and give that specification to the boys at the spring shop. Locally, they want $50-$60 per spring and can usually do the job in one day. De-arching makes the spring effectively longer and can create an unusual shackle angle. In some cases the upper shackle pivot may have to be moved back an inch or two.

If your street rod runs coil springs at one or both ends, then the options for spring choice are a little different. In the case of a Mustang-type suspension, the springs are usually ordered at the time you buy the suspension kit. If the springs come from the junk yard, remember that not all Mustang IIs or Pintos came with the same springs. Later-model models and those with air conditioning or the V-6 engine used heavier springs. The best recommendation for spring strength in these cases will probably come from the manufacturer of the suspension kit.

When you go looking for coil springs in the junkyard, keep in mind the formula for coil spring stiffness (more fascinating formulas), which is as follows:

Stiffness equals the diameter of the spring wire taken to the fourth power, times a constant (for a steel spring), divided by eight times the number of active coils, times the diameter of the spring taken to the third power.

Written out, it looks like this:

$$\text{Stiffness} = W^4 \times C / 8 \times N \times D^3$$

A couple of things about the formula. First, very small increases in the diameter of the coil wire make large changes in spring stiffness. Second, by cutting the number of coils you make a coil spring stiffer, not softer (the number of coils is on the bottom of the

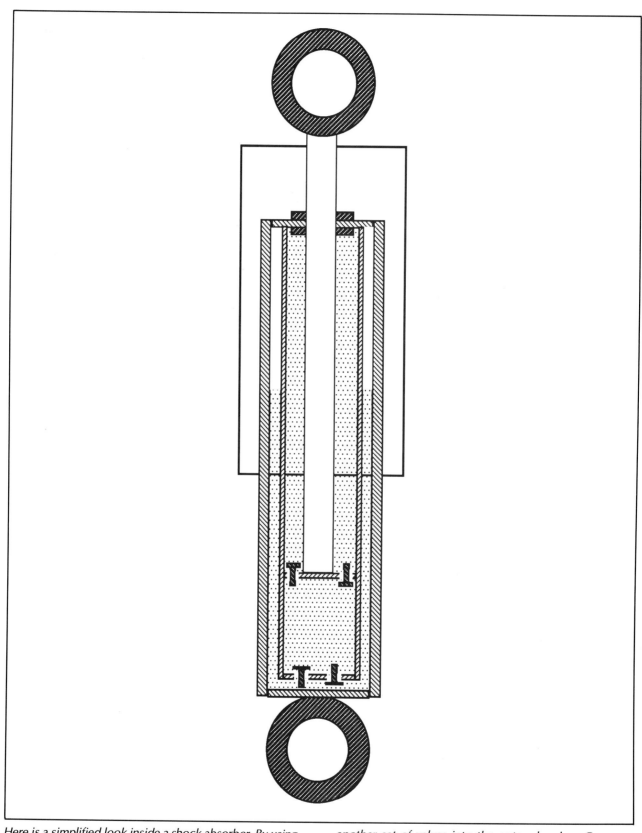

Here is a simplified look inside a shock absorber. By using different valves on the piston head, different compression and rebound rates are attained. As the piston head and rod move down into the cylinder, oil is forced through another set of valves into the outer chamber. Gas pressurized shocks pressurize the oil in the shock to prevent aerating the oil under heavy use.

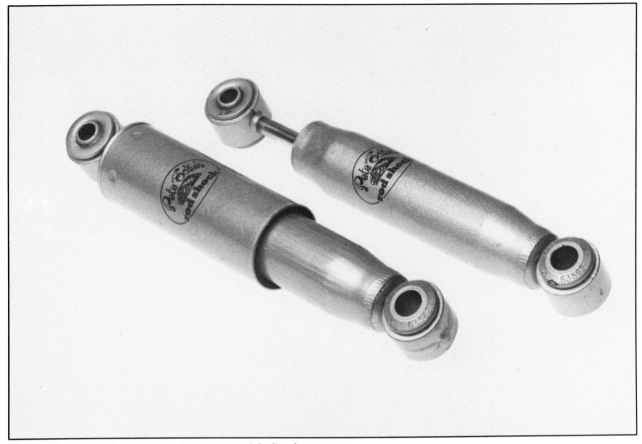

These tubular shocks are offered in two models for the front and rear of many street rods. Pete and Jake's

formula). Third, small changes in the diameter of the spring itself result in relatively large increases in stiffness. As the spring gets bigger it also gets softer.

It's probably time for a disclaimer and warning label in bold type:

A compressed coil spring stores enormous energy. Enough energy to kill and enough to tear your face off. You must know what you're doing and use the correct tools when removing and installing coil springs.

So, now you know that "cutting a coil" on your '48 Ford will make the car lower and the spring stiffer. If you want and need stiffer springs to prevent bottoming, that's OK—just understand what's happening. You can shorten your own coil springs if you have a mind to experiment. Get the spring safely out of the car and build a spring compressor (heavy-duty components are needed here). The compressor must compress the spring and keep it centered as well. Now, put the compressed spring in the oven at 400deg F for a few minutes. With luck and persistence you can create a spring that is shorter without changing the spring rate.

If the coil springs on your car wrap around a coil-over shock, then choosing the right springs is a lot easier. Most coil-over manufacturers offer charts

of estimated weights. You need to merely match the weight at each end of your vehicle to the appropriate length and pick out the right spring from the large number available.

Most manufacturers suggest that if in doubt, you should err on the softer, not the stiffer, side. These same manufacturers usually offer technical assistance in the choice of both springs and shocks for your car. Like the shock, the coil spring should never bottom out or "coil bind." This stresses the metal and causes fatigue, so be sure the coil springs aren't too long for the job.

When you order coil springs for the coil-overs, you need to consider the angle of the coil-over. As the coil-over moves from vertical to horizontal the effective strength of the spring is reduced. For example, at a 20deg lean, the effective spring rate is only 88 percent of the original rating. In order to get a true 200lb/in rate at a 20deg lean you would need to use a 227lb/in spring.

Some of the charts offered by the spring manufacturers have already compensated for lean. You need to ask if the chart assumes a 30deg lean angle. That way, if 200lb/in is what you need in the rear of your roadster, then 200lb/in is what you will get. Charts are offered by spring manufacturers and in the back of this book to help you find the proper corrected spring rate needed at any angle of lean.

Springs are very specific to a particular car. Don't ever swap the springs from one car to another because they look about the same. When you buy the coils to go along with your coil-overs, ask about a return policy. Some manufacturers will exchange the coils if the pair you bought turned out to be too stiff or too soft.

Hands-On

If the suspension in your new rod is a Mustang unit or subframe, then mounting shocks and springs is no problem. In most other cases you will need to move the suspension through its full range of motion. Without a spring or shock in place, most suspension can be moved easily from full bump to full extension. With a leaf spring suspension, you may need to take out all but the main leaf and then move the suspension from bump stop to full exten-

sion in order to check the dimensions for the new shock absorbers.

When you weld on the shock mountings, remember that a lot of force is transmitted through these mounts. If you're mounting coil-overs, then the entire weight of the car is supported by the shock mountings. In particular, the upper and lower mountings must be perfectly parallel (in the case of double-eye type mountings), or additional loads are transmitted to the mounts. Urethane bushings are available for the eye end of most shocks; it's a tougher material and also transmits less noise to the chassis and ultimately the body of the car. Many premium shocks come with urethane bushings.

Weld or attach the shock mounts so that two-thirds of the movement is available on compression and be sure that the suspension stop will stop the axle or the A-frame before the shock absorber does.

Though the finished car may not ride like a Cadillac (you probably don't *want* it to ride like a Cadillac), it doesn't have to ride like a lumber wagon either.

Chapter 7

Engine and Transmission Installation

Introduction

So after a lot of work, you've got the frame finished, the suspension bolted on, and you're ready to drop in the engine. As you study the frame sitting on the rack in your garage, you may start to wonder—just where does the engine go and how exactly are you going to mount it in the frame?

Theory

Where Does All This Stuff Go?

With any luck, you figured out most of this during the planning stage. By setting the engine farther back (within reason) you transfer more of the weight to the rear wheels. Though you probably won't achieve a fifty-fifty weight distribution without going to an Altered style engine location, moving the engine as little as 2 or 3in farther back can make a big difference in weight distribution.

The engine should be centered in the frame, between the two side rails. Though Detroit often offsets the engine slightly to the right, that probably isn't a good idea for your street rod. Detroit does it to compensate for the weight of the driver, and to make room for the steering. Street rodders do better to keep the engine centered in the frame, without any compensation or offset to one side.

The engine is the single, heaviest part of the car. In order to keep a nice low center of gravity and make your street rod go around corners like a Porsche, you might want to get all that weight nice and low in the frame. The concept is sound, though you have to remember that the bottom of the oil pan is one of the most vulnerable parts of your street rod. In the end, it's kind of like a Limbo contest—you can only go so low!

Once you've decided on a position, you need to think about the mounts themselves. Nearly all modern engines are mounted to the frame by three engine mounts. The two front mounts handle the bulk of the weight and also handle the enormous torque generated by a modern V-8. They told us in school that for every action there is an opposite reaction. The three hundred horses and 400lb-ft of torque that are generated on a hard launch are

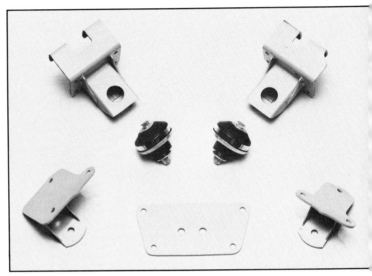

In the old days, my friends and I made our own motor mount brackets by carefully heating and bending steel plate heavy enough to make battleships out of. Today, you just pick up the phone and order a nice kit like this from Chassis Engineering, then drop a small-block into a 1940-48 Chevy. Chassis Engineering

Installing an engine and transmission means getting everything level—or at least knowing how far from level it is. It's all made much easier with a few common tools like these.

Slipping a small-block into a Model A frame is certainly facilitated with a nice mounting kit like these front and rear mounts from Pete and Jake's. The bracket running between the mounts is homemade and helps to hold the two mounts in place while all the measurements are checked.

A small-block engine bolted into a Model A frame. Note the tube running across the frame, a good way to check engine position and make sure it is level.

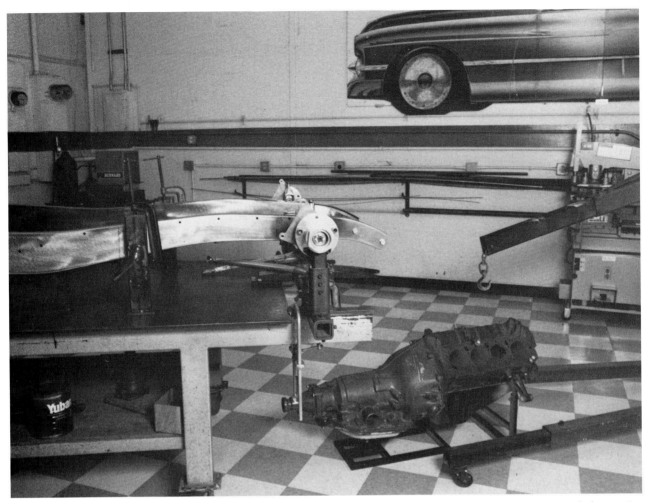

Here the same 1933-34 Ford chassis is almost ready for an engine installation. The rack mounted under the engine is a great aid in mounting engine mounts and the engine itself.

transmitted to and through the chassis by only three points—so they had better be good ones.

In particular, consider the structural integrity of the mount design. Triangles are good, especially if they're made from strong tubular steel. Flat plate that comes out from the rails to meet the engine, without any supporting members, isn't so good.

Buying and Making Engine Mounts

In days of old, it was often necessary to make or modify your engine mounts. Today, a variety of mounts and mount kits are available. For both large- and small-block Chevy engines, mount kits that use a factory style mount can be ordered, or you can order mounts that use a single bolt through a urethane bushing.

The simple, factory style pad mount offers good isolation from vibration along with ready availability. The triangular "street rod" mounts that utilize the urethane bushing allow very little flex and thus transmit more vibration through to the chassis of the car (and to the occupants of the car). These mounts allow so little flex that the engine becomes an "almost-stressed member" of the chassis.

When buying or building a rear mount, keep in mind that the transmission may need to come out at a later date—so be sure to leave a way for the cross-member or part of it to be unbolted and dropped out of the way. The rear mount itself should probably be a factory-style mount.

Hands-On

Setting the engine and transmission in the frame and mounting it correctly is made much easier with a small rack. The rack can be a fairly simple affair, just strong enough to hold the engine and transmission up off the table. By making it a little short, blocks and shims can be used to do the final positioning for engine height and angle. Without the rack or engine stand, you'll be wrestling with an engine dangling on a chain, trying to figure the location and the angle of the dangle—all while trying to keep the engine from moving.

The engine has been set down between the rails. The front-to-rear location is determined by the firewall—most builders place the engine as far back as possible in order to keep as much weight on the back wheels as possible.

Larry Sergejeff mounts a water pump and fan so he knows for sure where to put the radiator saddle.

As the engine drops, lower clearance between the fan (and lower pulley) and the front cross-member can become a problem.

As a good way to check the height of the engine and to make sure it's the same height from one side to another, some shops run a piece of square tubing across the frame rails and then put two bolts into two of the holes for the front timing cover or water pump.

You might want to bolt on a water pump and fan (if you're using a belt-driven fan) before deciding on the final location for the engine. It makes a good double-check of engine location and the available room between the water pump, fan, and radiator.

As stated earlier, you need at least 5in of clearance between the bottom of the oil pan and terra firma. If you are setting the engine and transmission into a bare frame, you need to know the location of the firewall. You probably want to set the engine as far back as the firewall will allow. The engine should be set in the center of the rails, at the height you've determined to be correct.

When it comes to the correct angle for the engine, most shops dip the engine down at the back by 1 or 2deg. Some builders like to mount the intake manifold and then put a level across the carburetor mounting base to ensure that the engine is mounted so that the carburetor is level or nearly level. The next question is: What about the driveline angles?

Many of the cars to come out of the Boyd shop are equipped with these triangulated motor mounts. The design is simple and very, very strong. The urethane bushings transmit a little more vibration but they also hold the engine so solidly that it adds to the strength of the chassis.

137

The tape measure shows just over 5in of clearance between the bottom of the pan and the ground—probably the minimum anyone wants for the street.

Having the centerline of the frame marked on the table makes it easy to use a T-square to make sure the rear of the transmission is centered between the frame rails.

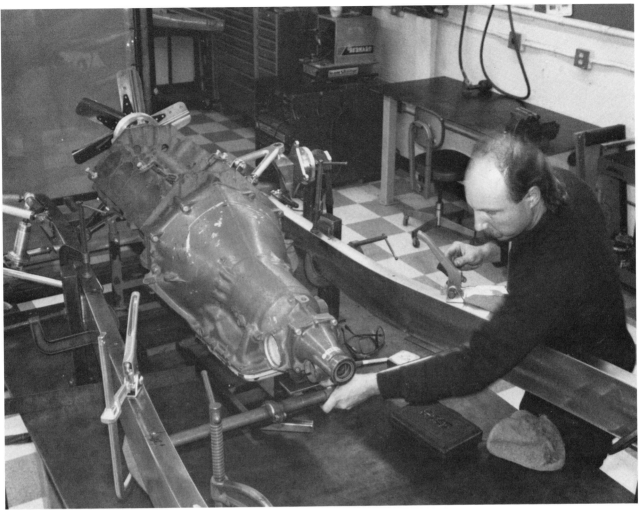

Larry checks the rear motor mount (transmission mount) for correct fit. Note that the mount has a drop-out section in the center to aid later transmission removal. The mount is made from the same 0.120in wall, mild steel tubing used throughout the chassis.

Larry likes to set the engine at a one- or two-degree angle (transmission lower). The drop-out section of the mount is just two pairs of simple, bolt-together flanges.

A tape measure is used at the front to make sure the engine is set in the very center of the frame rails.

After the engine is correctly set for position and angle, these front mount tabs can be welded to the frame.

Figuring the Angle of the Dangle

A good way to start an argument among a group of street rodders might be to ask each how to correctly set the driveline angles. Even among professionals, there are some very different opinions. Some say the pinion angle (the angle of the centerline of the pinion shaft as seen from a side view) should match the angle of the engine and transmission, while others insist that the two angles should be different by at least 1 or 2deg.

Jim Petrykowski, a man who builds everything from very short wheelbase Anglias to large and long fat-fendered Fords, feels that the only time the angles should be the same is in the case of short-wheelbase cars with gobs of horsepower. Professional shops have a long, telescoping steel rod that can be bolted into the engine's main bearing caps and bolted securely to the rear-end housing. When setting up a dragster chassis or serious pro-street Anglia, that special rod is used as a means of putting everything in one straight line—so it is better able to transfer enormous amounts of horsepower and torque.

In the case of more common street cars and street rods, the engine "centerline" is usually at a different height than the pinion. Jim likes to have a difference of 1 or 2deg between the angle of the

Once the engine is mounted, it's time to measure up a driveshaft. Larry bottoms the front yoke and then backs it out 1in, and uses that measurement (cap centerline to cap centerline) for the driveshaft.

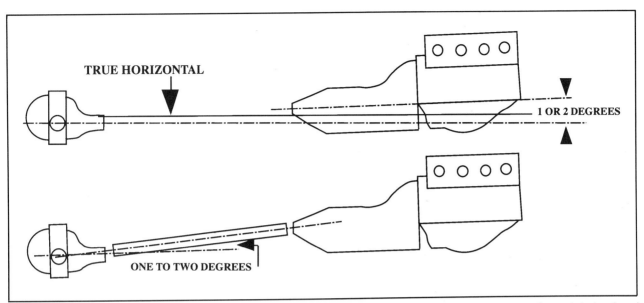

TRUE HORIZONTAL

1 OR 2 DEGREES

ONE TO TWO DEGREES

When there is no driveshaft to install, the pinion angle can be adjusted to point down one or two degrees more than the engine centerline—at ride height, of course. Not everyone agrees with this, but this setup does work. Mount the engine where it needs to be (so the carb is level and the rear isn't lower by more than two degrees), then mount a driveshaft and adjust the pinion angle to be one or two degrees different than the driveshaft angle.

Back to the '41 Ford frame at Metal Fab. Here the Pete and Jake's engine mount has been welded to the frame. Note the simple, triangulated design. The mount itself is a factory GM piece.

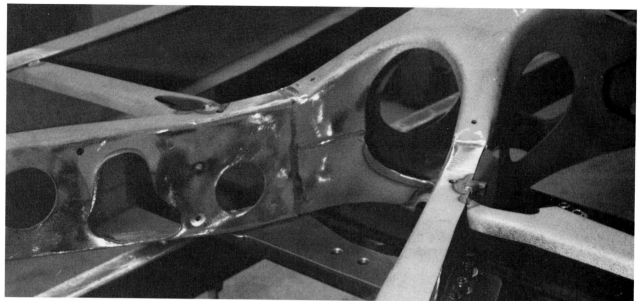

The rear mount in the '41 Ford frame is also from Pete and Jake's, just a simple plate that bolts to the original X-member. The X-member has been "modified" to provide clearance for the Turbo Hydro 350 transmission.

Here the engine is set down onto the mounts.

Close-up shows the factory pad-type engine mount bolted to the P and J mount.

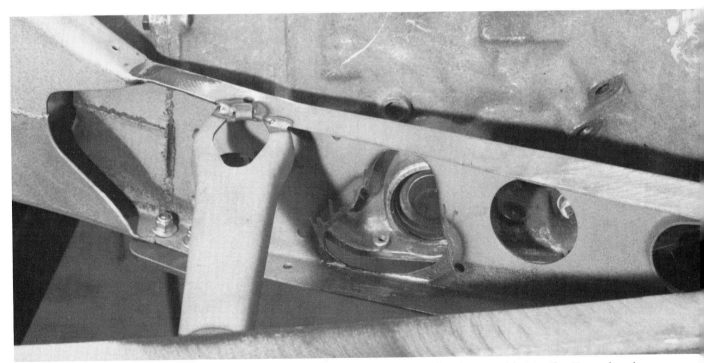

Another close-up, showing why it was necessary to "modify" the X-member for the automatic transmission. Note that the short cross-member—normally held in place by tabs—has been welded to the X-member for extra strength.

Another Metal Fab job. Petrykowski, Sr., guides a small-block going into a Model A frame. The dummy engine is equipped with a water pump and lower pulley.

A little guidance is needed to line up the rear motor mount.

The front mounts are a unique tubular design, short, simple, and strong.

The rear mount is a unique and somewhat elegant Metal Fab design. Note again the drop-out for later transmission removal.

engine and transmission, and the angle of the pinion (in side view).

As already mentioned, in the top view, the rear end often has an offset to one side. Jim usually leaves this offset intact, assuming that the dimensions of the finished rear-end housing will place the driveshaft in the center of the driveshaft-tunnel. In the top view, then, the centerline of the pinion and the engine are usually offset slightly but the two centerlines are parallel.

In the side view, Jim prefers to work with a driveshaft in place. After years of building cars, he feels that the angle between the pinion and the driveshaft is the most important: "When I can, I just put a driveshaft in place between the engine and the rear end and move the rear-end housing until I have the pinion at the same angle as the driveshaft. Then I point the pinion down another 1 or 2deg."

When there is no driveshaft to mount between the transmission and rear end, Jim sets the pinion angle at the same angle as the engine—minus 1 or 2deg (nose pointed down). The idea is to make the U-joints "work" as they rotate. If everything were in perfect alignment the cross shaft would always rest against the same needle bearings in the cap. When the angles are different by a few degrees the cross shaft will walk around the caps, rotating the needles and spreading the load and wear as it does so. A difference of a degree or two is also a good way to dampen vibration and harmonics that can build in the driveline and resonate through the car.

What you want is a drivetrain where all the components are securely mounted. Just as important, you want all those components located in such a way that wear and vibration are kept to an absolute minimum.

An overview of the same Model A frame. Always put a water pump and even a fan on mock-up engines so you know how much room is left between the fan and the radiator.

Chapter 8

Wheels and Tires

Introduction

The wheels for your street rod are nearly as important as the engine. Put a set of slotted mags on a modern smoothie and what've you got? Likewise, a set of Boyd's Wheels just don't fit on an early style Track-T or Deuce Roadster.

More than style is at stake here, though. Your choice of wheels and tires will help determine how the car handles, turns, and stops. To buy the right wheels you need to know what will bolt onto the hub and also what will fit under the fenders.

Theory

Wheel Terms for the Wheel World

Understanding wheels means understanding seven terms. Let's roll through them one at a time.

Known as the Posie II, this new-wave design seems to be moving when it's standing still. The two-piece wheel used a billet center that was cut on CNC equipment and then mated to the rim and finally polished to a high shine.

Bolt circle: The bolt circle is the diameter of the bolt circle, usually preceded by the number of lugs, either four or five for most automotive uses. Thus, 4 x 4.5 means the rim has four bolt holes and that the diameter of the bolt circle is 4½in.

If you wonder how to figure the bolt circle diameter on a wheel with five studs, there's a simple formula. First, you need to know the distance between two adjacent studs (the centerline distance), then multiply that figure by 1.7013.

Hub diameter: Hub diameter is the diameter of the hole in the center of the wheel.

Rim width: This is simply the distance across the rim—measured on the inside of the rim flange.

Wheel backspacing: Wheel backspacing is the distance between the wheel's mounting surface and the rim's inside flange.

Wheel front spacing: Yup, it's the distance from the wheel mounting surface to the rim's *outer* flange.

Offset: This is where it gets confusing. Offset is a measure of how far *offset* the center of the rim is from the wheel mounting surface. A "chrome reverse" rim is one with a lot of offset to the outside while many modern front-wheel-drive cars have a lot of offset to the inside. Whether offset to the outside of the car should be referred to as positive or negative depends on whom you talk to. We won't talk about negative or positive any further. If you had a rim width of 6in and 3in of back spacing, then that rim would have zero offset—the wheel mounting surface is right in the middle of the rim.

Wheel load capacity: This refers to the amount of weight the wheel can safely withstand.

In addition to the above, you also need to consider the type of lug nut used by a particular rim and whether a particular rim allows clearance for calipers and (occasionally) large-finned brake drums.

Wheel Definitions

Before we had fuel injection or radial tires, the wheels on most hot rods were either stock, chrome reversed, or "wires." Today, the possibilities are almost endless. Everything from steelies with center caps to Boyd billet wheels can be found on modern

The Cast Hammer is one of the new cast designs to roll out of the casting department at Boyd's Wheels.

The Tri-Fan is another billet wheel from Boyd's. The three-blade design was so well accepted that Boyd's now has a new model, the Deuce, featuring only two spokes. These are the designs that truly call for the strength of forged, 6061 T6 aluminum. The open designs show off a polished caliper to good effect.

The Sequal 40 is a two-piece wheel utilizing a forged center, available either polished or brushed. The small "ring" floating halfway between the hub and the rim adds a nice touch to the design.

street rods. What follows is a short explanation of some of the terms used to describe those modern wheels.

Most aluminum or mag style wheels are considered to be either a two-piece or a three-piece wheel. The two-piece wheels use a center section welded or bolted to a one-piece rim. Three-piece wheels bolt (usually) the center section to the two pieces that make up the rim.

True billet wheels (at least those from Boyd's) use a solid billet of forged, 6061 T6 aluminum as the center section of the wheel. These billets are then cut on CNC machines to create the spokes and designs and are later welded to the rim. But not all billet wheels are actually billet—forged material is much stronger than a simple casting, and 6061 T6 (6061 refers to the makeup of the alloy and T6 refers to the hardness) is about as good as it gets. So if you want the very best, make sure your centers are made from *forged* aluminum.

Cast wheels use an aluminum casting as the center section of the wheel. The spokes are usually part of the casting pattern. Thus a cast wheel requires less machining and can be sold for a lower price. Certain designs—like the new two-spoke Boyd design—require the enormous strength of forged aluminum, though in most other cases the cast material has adequate strength. Although they might not be up to the strength of a billet wheel, there's nothing *wrong* with a cast-aluminum wheel.

High-quality wheels have the center section welded to the rim along the entire surface where the two parts meet. And any wheel worth its weight in

The Fluted Star is a cast wheel with a nice simple design, available in 15in and 16in from 5in to 9in wide and with backspacing from 2in to almost 7in.

polished billet will have radial and lateral runout held to less than 0.010in.

Tires Defined

Understanding tires means understanding just a few more definitions:

Aspect ratio: This is the section height divided by the section width. The smaller the number, the "wider" the tire, relative to its height. A 205/75R15 is a 15in tire with an aspect ratio of 75. A 205/50R15 is a 15in tire with an aspect ratio of 50. This second tire is *fifty percent* as high as it is wide.

There are a few more numbers embossed into the sidewall of your tires. Among all those numbers and codes is speed rating. This is a letter code and indicates the highest speed the tire is designed to withstand.

Rating Code	Maximum Speed
N	87mph
P	93mph
Q	99mph
R	106mph
S	113mph
T	118mph
H	130mph
V	149mph
Z	Speeds in excess of 149mph

Sometimes the speed rating is integrated into the tire size, as in P205/60SR15. The P indicates passenger car use, the S is the speed rating (up to 113mph).

This Euro 74 is a spoked design, somehow old and new at the same time. A forged two-piece wheel, the sizes range from 14in to 17in in widths from 6in to 11in.

Hands-On

Buying Wheels and Tires for Your New Ride

Everyone wants big fat tires, yet you can't put a 225/60/15 on a 4in wide rim. Without enough rim width the tire never flattens. Wear and handling are affected as well. Tire and wheel choices have to be integrated. Each tire size has a recommended rim width and a published width and height. Minimum rim sizes for a given size of tire vary slightly between tire brands and even models. If there's any doubt, check the individual tire manufacturer's charts (available at the tire store) to be sure the rim you've got is wide enough for the tire you want to mount.

Tire manufacturers talk about Plus 1 and Plus 2 fitments. A Plus 1 is a case where you go from a 14in to a 15in tire and keep the overall diameter the same. For example, a P205/70SR14 is the same diameter as a P215/60R15 in the Michelin line. The difference, of course, is that the 15in tire with its lower aspect ratio is wider and has less sidewall. The wider face and shorter sidewall affect both the look of the tire and the way it handles.

When you consider the size of the rear tires for your new street rod, be sure to include the diameter in your figuring. Roadsters and many early cars, especially hiboys, look good with some pretty tall tires on the back. If you plan to run some tall rubber on the back of your hiboy, remember that a tall tire acts like a higher rear gear ratio. A relatively high 3.10:1 gear ratio combined with a tall rear tire measuring 34in in diameter will have the engine turning only 1839rpm at 60mph. The resulting mileage might be great although the performance will be

Here a rim is being measured for backspacing—the distance from the mounting surface to the outer edge of the rim. When considering backspace, remember that the tire bulges out past the edge of the rim.

Rim width is measured between the inner lips of the rim.

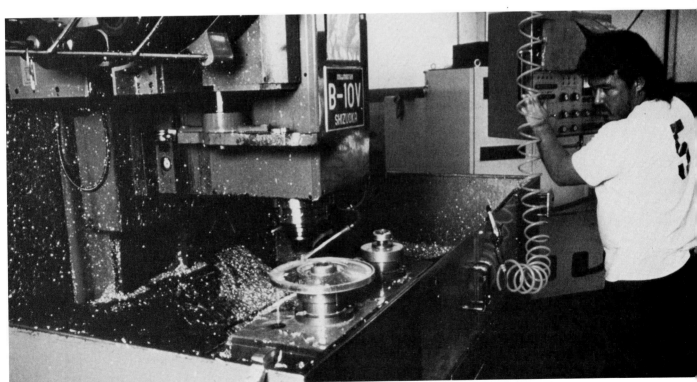

At Boyd's Wheels, Don Oliver and the B-10V begin cutting the actual design into the wheel center. Different cutting bits, needed to cut out the complex wheel design, are stored in the large wheel at upper left. Customers can even create their own designs mated to almost any width rim and offset.

A close-up view of the B-10V used at Boyd's Wheels. Cutting each wheel center requires a number of different operations, and a number of different tool bits.

Wheels are stacked in the assembly and welding area at Boyd's Wheels. The rims are heated, then dropped over the wheel centers and then cooled. After a runout check (held to less than 0.010in), the wheels move to the automatic welder.

150

Three-piece wheels have become the minor part of the Boyd's Wheels business. Here a series of centers waits to be mated with a two-piece rim to create a new wheel.

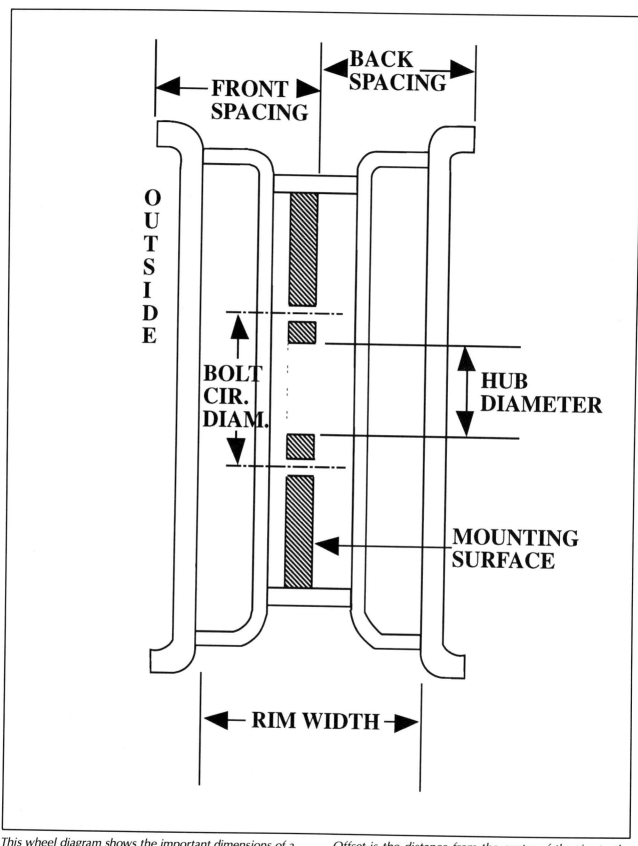

This wheel diagram shows the important dimensions of a wheel. They're the dimensions you need to keep in mind as you make plans to buy wheels and tires for your car.

Offset is the distance from the center of the rim to the mounting surface. This wheel has zero offset since the rim is centered over the mounting surface.

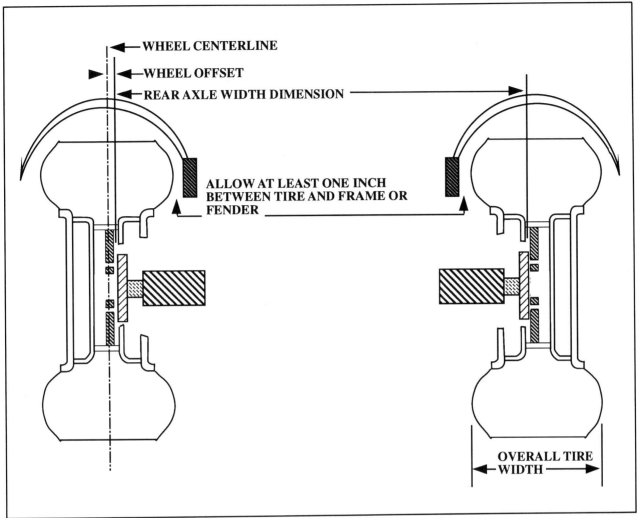

WHEEL CENTERLINE

WHEEL OFFSET

REAR AXLE WIDTH DIMENSION

ALLOW AT LEAST ONE INCH
BETWEEN TIRE AND FRAME OR
FENDER

OVERALL TIRE
WIDTH

A sketch like this will help you avoid confusion and ensure that you get the tire, wheel, and rear-end dimensions you need. If you are having a rear end cut to fit, then mount the tires on the rims (if possible) and set the rims up under the fenders, measuring from mounting flange to mounting flange. If you already have the rear end, then use the published width figures for your new tires plus the rear-end dimension to determine where the tires will end up without any offset. Use rim offset (the difference between the mounting surface and the center of the rim) to place the tires where you need them.

less than exhilarating. Take a look at the diameter/rpm chart and figure out what rpm the engine will be turning with a given tire diameter. Then decide if you need to reconsider either the tire or the gear ratio.

When you plan tires for your street rod there are just a few final pointers:

The correct look for some Bucket Ts includes monster tires at the rear and little motorcycle tires in front. It might look great, but it's a bit frightening when you consider that the front tires do most of the stopping and all of the turning. Yes, some of these cars have the engine set way back in the frame, but still. . .

There is a recommended load limit for each size and brand of tire—often stamped in the side of the tire and available from the manufacturer as well. Make sure you put enough rubber on the front of the

car to properly support the weight, stop the car, and negotiate it around the corner.

The other extreme offers a downside as well. As the tire grows in cross section, its ability to force water out from under the center of the tread becomes more and more limited. Hydroplaning down the highway in a pro-street coupe isn't much fun. When you buy that monster rubber, understand that you may have to sit out a few rainstorms or consider less-than-monster tires in a brand and model that offers good wet-weather traction.

Some tire manufacturers offer rain tires or all-season tires with good wet-weather operation. These tires feature tread designs with plenty of open area between the tread blocks so water has some-place to go and isn't trapped between the tread and the highway. Each tire model has a published sheet of characteristics. Before buying a particular tire, ask to see these specification and information sheets so you know what kind of tire you're buying.

How you use all these measurements to buy rims that correctly fit your street rod depends on your situation. If you're putting new wheels and tires on an existing car, then you need to start measuring from wheel mounting flange to wheel mounting flange on the axle.

Always use the mounting surface as your baseline measurement. You also need to determine available tire clearance—depending on the location of the frame rail and inner fender on one side and the outer fender lip on the other. Make a sketch to avoid confusion. How much tire can you get under the fender (tire widths are published for each brand and size)? Now, how wide a rim do you need in order to mount that particular tire size? Finally, what kind of offset does the wheel need to have in order to center that tire between the fender and the frame rail?

If you're building your car from scratch (like one of Mom's cakes) then the rim you choose should be decided upon during the planning process. You need to figure how much tire you want (or can stuff under the fender), how wide a rim you need to mount that tire, where that tire should be positioned—and then work backwards. Will you have a rear end narrowed to your specs or have you got a rear axle that needs to be matched with the correct rims?

As discussed in chapter 4, many builders will have trouble finding a rear end that fits without narrowing or one that works without some extra offset (to the inside) on the rim. The advantage of having an axle assembly narrowed is that you get what you want—an axle exactly the right width. The other advantage is that you don't have to order odd wheels with a lot of offset or backspacing.

The subject of wheels and tires is just like everything else: it seems simple until you look closely at it, and suddenly there are a million choices that all seem pretty confusing. The only way to clear up the confusion is by learning more about the topic of tires and then using that knowledge to make a decision that weighs cost, appearance, and performance.

Sources

Boyd's Wheels
8402 Cerritos Avenue
Stanton, CA 90680

Chassis Engineering
119 N Second
West Branch, IA 52358

Engineered Components Inc
PO Box 2361
Vernon, CT 06066

Fat Man Fabrications
8621 C Fairview Road
Hwy 218
Charlotte, NC 28227

Heidt's Hot Rod Shop
5420 Newport Drive, #49
Rolling Meadows, IL 60008

Hot Rods by Boyd
8372 Monroe Avenue
Stanton, CA 90680

JFZ Brake Components
440 East Easy Street
Simi Valley, CA 93065

Just a Hobby
531 Schrock
Columbus, OH 43229

Magnum Axle Company
PO Box 2342
Oakhurst CA 93644

Metal Fab
1453 91st Avenue NE
Blaine, MN 55434
Attn: Jim Petrykowski

Morrison Performance
Art Morrison Ent.
5301 Eighth Street E
Fife, WA 98424

P & J
6262 Riverside Drive
Danville, VA 24541

Pete and Jake's
11924 Blue Ridge Ext.
Grandview, MO 64030

Posies
219 N Duke Street
Hummelstown, PA 17036

Redneck
RR2, Box 174
Fort Branch, IN 47648

SAC
1815 Orangethorpe, Unit C
Anaheim, CA 92801

Street Rod Manufacturing Co.
9635 Hwy 85, #2
Littleton, CO 80125

Super Bell Axle Company
2885 S Chestnut Avenue
Fresno, CA 93725

Total Cost Involved (TCI)
1416 W Brooks Street
Ontario, CA 91762

Wilwood
4580 Calle Alto
Camarillo, CA 93010

Shocks and Coil-Overs
Aldan Shock Absorber Co.
646 E 219th Street
Carson, CA 90745

Carrera
5412 New Peachtree Road
Atlanta, GA 30341

Pro Shocks
1865 S Beaver Ridge Circle
Norcross, GA 30071

Safe Disposal and Recycling of Parts and Chemicals

One of the most difficult problems in repairing or restoring any vehicle is the question of what to do with the old parts and poisonous fluids you inevitably generate. Everybody knows these days that two of our largest environmental concerns are the related ills of landfill overuse and groundwater contamination. Unfortunately, our interest in environmental problems far outstrips our current ability to find answers to them.

While repairing or restoring your vehicle, there are several components and fluids that can actually be recycled, such as batteries, motor oil, electrical components, brake pads, and more. Take advantage of the recycling effort.

There are many more components and fluids that cannot be recycled, however. The best you can do with these hazardous wastes is to control the spread of the hazard. Check with your local pollution control agency or your county government for hazardous waste collection sites where you can dispose of these parts and fluids.

Parts

Actual pieces of mechanical junk are generally more of a pain than a danger to dispose of. Assuming that the pieces aren't filled with fluid or particularly greasy, metal parts will sit happily inert in a landfill and actually decompose over time—albeit a long, long time. Yet, some plastic and rubber pieces release a number of carcinogenic chemicals as they decompose. If possible, you should bring big metal parts to a local junkyard; often yards will accept these pieces for their scrap value and sometimes melt them down to be recycled.

Batteries

Old vehicle batteries are like environmental time bombs just waiting to explode. The average vehicle battery contains more than 18lb of toxic metals, and the chemicals inside can burst through the plastic shell or seep through cracks and leak onto your floor. And everyone has one or two old batteries laying around in a corner of their garage or workshop.

Fortunately, batteries are easy to dispose of and the cores can be recycled by the manufacturers to make new batteries. In many states, shops that sell batteries are required by law to accept old batteries free of charge and see to their safe disposal. Some responsible shops even reinforce this by giving you a rebate when buying a new battery if you bring in the old battery.

Tires

Tires are a well-known dumping hazard, and methods for their disposal have been well-developed in almost every state. In the past when you went to dispose of your old tires at a tire shop or landfill, the typical response was to say that you can't dump your tires there, which is ultimately the wrong answer, since many people just get frustrated and toss them by the side of the road or in vacant lots.

Most states today have mandatory tire buy-back laws for dealers and shops. These laws typically have regulations that require tire dealers to accept used tires for disposal, usually with a small fee attached.

Electrical Components

Core parts of many electrical components can be recycled by the manufacturers to build new units. Alternators, generators, starter motors, and other electrical components fall into this category, and many shops will offer a rebate on your new part when you bring in the old one for recycling. Take advantage of such an arrangement.

Brake Pads

Brake pad cores can also be recycled by the manufacturers, and in many states, shops that sell pads are required by law to accept old pads free of charge and see to their recycling or safe disposal. This is especially important with nonmetallic, asbestos brake pads since asbestos is a powerful carcinogen.

When replacing asbestos pads, never blow away old brake dust with your face nearby as it simply provides you with easy-to-inhale airborne asbestos dust. Instead, use a moist cloth to wipe it away and dispose of the cloth.

Exhaust System Components

Not surprisingly, all of the exhaust system components that you route the engine exhaust through become caked with carcinogens and pollutants over time. The only way to safely dispose of used exhaust pipes, mufflers, and catalytic converters is to bring them to a hazardous waste collection site or to contact your local pollution control agency for other alternative sites.

Fluids

The best rule of thumb as you work with chemicals and fluids is to remember that if you can smell it, it's bad news. And the stronger the odor, the more dangerous it is—both to your immediate health and to the atmosphere and groundwater. Cleaners, paints, and all oil-derived liquids are the big things to watch out for. Dumped carelessly by the wayside, these toxic chemicals will quickly work their way into the water cycle and return to haunt us all.

The easiest solution, of course, is not to generate any more of these wastes than necessary in the first place. Except for motor oil, the greatest volume of volatile chemicals is generated by cleaning, not the actual changing of a car's fluids. It's best to start off with the mildest cleaners possible at first—soap and water can, in fact, do a lot of work—not just for the environment's sake but because these are also the easiest on the vehicle itself.

You will inevitably generate some hazardous material no matter what you do, however. Things like spray cleaners and naptha, for example—real health and environmental nightmares—are just too convenient to realistically swear off of completely. The trick is simply to catch as much of these fluids as possible after use, and to keep them tightly covered in plastic, glass, or metal containers until you can safely get rid of them. Leaving pans of cleaners uncovered sends these toxins directly into the atmosphere through evaporation, so keep them covered at all times.

Caked grease and ruined rags should also be kept tightly wrapped up in a cool place and disposed of along with actual fluids—they're simply volatiles that are currently trapped in solid form. And beware of the fire hazard of these rags.

All toxins should be kept separated since cross contamination simply makes the disposal issue more complicated.

Motor Oil

Used motor oil poses a great threat to the environment—and to yourself, as it contains carcinogens. Many states prohibit putting used motor oil in the trash or disposing of it in landfills.

Fortunately, however, motor oil can be recycled and used as fuel for ships, furnaces, and other things. In many states, shops that sell oil or provide oil changes are required by law to collect used motor oil for recycling.

Some counties offer curbside recycling of used motor oil, so check with your county government. These recycling programs sometimes have strict rules on how the used oil must be stored if they will take it for recycling; some want it stored only in plastic containers while others require glass jars, so be sure to ask.

You must also be certain to keep your used motor oil pure and not mix it with other fluids for disposal. If the used oil is contaminated with even minute traces of brake fluid or coolant, the entire batch in the collection tank will be ruined.

Antifreeze and Coolant

The main ingredient in antifreeze and coolants is ethylene glycol, a chemical that can be reconditioned in wastewater treatment systems. Small amounts of used antifreeze—1 gallon or so—can thus be safely disposed of in your home's sanitary sewer system when mixed with large amounts of water.

You should never dispose of antifreeze in storm sewers or septic systems as these do not run through the wastewater treatment system and the ethylene glycol will eventually contaminate the groundwater. Antifreeze dumped into a septic system will also destroy the bacteria in the system that septic tanks rely on to operate.

Parts Cleaners

The old-fashioned parts cleaner fluids that worked like magic in removing years of oil and grime from your vehicle parts also removed layers of your own skin and seeped directly into your liver, where they definitely didn't do you any good. When disposing of these old parts cleaners, first read the label on the container. If the product is labelled as being flammable, combustible , or contains any solvents such as petroleum distillates or aromatic hydrocarbons, then it must be disposed of at a hazardous waste collection site.

If the product is a liquid and does not contain any solvents, it can usually be disposed of in a sanitary sewer system after being mixed with large quantities of water. Never pour it down a storm sewer or into a septic system since the liquids will not be treated but will instead seep directly into our groundwater.

Today several alternative parts cleaners are readily available and easy on you and the environment while still scrubbing away all the oil and grease. Check them out.

There is also one other option: Never underestimate the power of hot water, soap, and scrubbing.

Gasoline

Gasoline is one of the most dangerous fluids around your house or workshop because it is extremely volatile.

Often times, most waste gas is either contaminated or old. If it has been contaminated with paint or other soluble contaminants, it cannot be reconditioned. Check with your county for a hazardous waste collection site.

Stale gas can be used after adding one of the many reconditioning agents on the market. However, many people prefer not to risk their vehicle's engine and use the stale gas in a lawn mower or other small gas engine instead.

Alignment Guide

The Pete and Jake's catalog (a great source of general building information) suggests you run five degrees positive caster for straight axles in Ford street rods.

Jim Petrykowski suggests that straight axle cars run the following:
Caster, five or six degrees, positive
Camber, one degree positive
Toe-in, 3/32 to 1/8in

He further suggests that if the car is small and the driver is heavy, the alignment should be done with the driver in the vehicle. You may also want to level out the coil-overs (if possible) with the driver in the car.

Gary Heidt's instructions for Mustang II systems include the following specs:
Caster, one degree positive
Camber, one-half degree positive
Toe-in, 1/8in + or − 1/8in

Individual systems like the Heidt Superide and some others should be adjusted per the instructions that come with the kit.

Remember, street rods vary a great deal in their size, weight, weight distribution, wheels and suspension—these "specs" are only starting points. You cannot adjust the camber on a straight axle without bending the axle at a front-end shop with special equipment. So unless it's way off, you pretty much just run what you've got.

In the case of Mustang II and some other independent suspensions, you can try more positive caster as a means of creating more directional stability and greater self-centering after a turn, though the trade-off is harder steering at slow speeds (only noticeable with manual steering). As a final note, some alignment shops and mechanics like to adjust the right front wheel with about 1/4 degree more positive caster as a means of compensating for road crown (the car tends to "pull" to the side with the least positive caster).

Coil-Over Angle

When mounting coil-overs, you need to correct the absolute spring rate to the effective spring rate depending on the degree of lean. For example, a 200lb/in spring mounted at a thirty degree angle has an effective rate of only 150lb/in. To get a true 200lb/in spring at a thirty degree lean, you need a spring rated at 266lb/in (266x.75 = 200).

Note that a few spring manufacturers have already corrected their spring rates and assume a thirty degree mounting—so be sure to ask.

Shock Angle:	10	15	20	25	30	35	40
Correction factor:	.96	.93	.88	.82	.75	.66	.59

RPM Chart

RPM at 60mph
Gear Ratios

Tire Diameters (in)	2.5	3.1	3.42	3.78	4.11	4.56	5.12
22	2292	2842	3135	3465	3768	4180	4694
24	2100	2605	2874	3176	3454	3832	4302
26	1939	2405	2653	2932	3188	3537	3972
28	1800	2233	3463	2723	2960	3284	3688
30	1680	2084	2300	2540	2763	3065	3442
32	1575	1954	2155	2382	2590	2874	3227
34	1482	1839	2029	2242	2440	2705	3037
36	1400	1739	1916	2118	2302	2555	2868

Index